"In this blend of memoir and rep[ortage the] writer surveys the eighty-eight independent and deeply unequal cities that make up the 'nation-state' of Los Angeles . . . The place that emerges is one of extreme luck, extreme misfortune, and no middle class, and yet, perhaps, not just 'a jumble of people any more than a song was a string of notes.'" —*The New Yorker*

"Los Angeles invites extreme forms of correspondence—love letters and hate mail—and Rosecrans Baldwin's *Everything Now* is a lush amalgam of both. In beautiful and concise prose, he maps a sun-drenched geography that we love to hate and hate to love. Baldwin cements his status as one of California's finest literary cartographers." —Myriam Gurba, author of *Mean*

"*Everything Now* is a genre-bending work of reportage and memoir that's been lauded as one of the best and most inventive books of the summer. It's a book that delights in the mysteries of the place." —Geoffrey Gagnon, *GQ*

"If you're not already under the odd spell that LA so often casts on even people who've never visited it, you'll feel the light brushing of that spell while reading these pages; if you find the whole idea of Los Angeles vaguely, indefinably revolting, Baldwin's anecdotes will make you seethe delectably with vicarious disapproval; and if you are indeed already bewitched by LA, you now have a new piece of required reading."
—Steve Donoghue, *Open Letters Review*

"It's precisely Los Angeles's fundamental ambiguity, its magnetic swirl of beauty and darkness, that makes books like Baldwin's worth writing, and reading. Put in your time in L.A. and eventually you'll feel the ambient sadness that Carey McWilliams discerned seventy-five years ago."

—Casey Schwartz, *Los Angeles Review of Books*

"Baldwin offers an amalgam of voices in the form of stories, conversations, and reflections that add up to a spectacular collage portrait of Los Angeles. The result is a daring and innovative excavation of the City of Angels as 'the Great American City-State.'"

—*Alta*

"Full of surprising facts and anecdotes, this is a compelling, thoroughly researched, and lovingly crafted chronicle of how Los Angeles came to be."

—Alexander Moran, *Booklist*

"A witty and imaginative survey of contemporary L.A. . . . This multifaceted, openhearted account reveals L.A. as a 'shifting mosaic of human potential' unlike any other place in the world."

—*Publishers Weekly*

"Despite reckoning with a litany of contemporary apocalypses, it remains a book levied with humor, including an inventive appropriation of Charles Bukowski's character Henry Chinaski, an exposé of the lampoonable greed of investment trusts that view human suffering as a once-in-a-lifetime opportunity to 'buy low,' and a hilarious depiction of a screenwriting team's meeting with Hollywood producers gone awry."

—Sean Hooks, *Full Stop*

"In a brisk and graceful style, Rosecrans Baldwin has produced a new and necessary guidebook for contemporary Los Angeles, one that captures the elusive and bewildering qualities of the beautiful sprawling nightmare so many of us call home. *Every-*

thing Now should be handed out to everyone who gets off a plane at LAX."

—Jim Gavin, author of *Middle Men* and creator of *Lodge 49*

"All the research, all the thinking and wandering and interviewing, that Rosecrans Baldwin did to get head and heart, arms and eyes, around greater Los Angeles sits barely beyond the sightlines of the beautiful storytelling, the unpacking of myth and memory, the narrative wrestling match with a place that has crushed so many other would-be interpreters. Baldwin tackles a city-state's sprawling past and present across great chunks of chronology and culture, and does it with grace and imagination. This book is a revelation."   —William Deverell, director, Huntington-USC Institute on California and the West

"With a novelist's eye and a searching curiosity, Rosecrans Baldwin has created a sprawling work that explores a place and its people, as well as culture, history, geography, and ecology. A feat of imagination that fed my mind, heart, and soul."

—Charles Yu, winner of the National Book Award for *Interior Chinatown*

"Rosecrans Baldwin's *Everything Now* is the rare work that understands L.A. for its sphinxlike inscrutability and complex history. It refuses to lapse into cheap stereotype or inherited cliché, yet remains skeptical of the cultish lure and sunbaked weirdness. This is the meticulously reported and three-dimensional contemporary history that the city needs."

—Jeff Weiss, editor in chief, *TheLAnd*

"I was born in Los Angeles and intend to die here—there's no place in the world I love more. I'm also constantly furious about the many ways it falls short of its promise. Rosecrans Baldwin has taken on the unwieldy task of portraying this unique, enormous city in all its overlapping, contradictory layers, and incredibly, he succeeds. With vivid stories and a ready knowledge of local literature and history, he captures the sunshine and noir of twenty-first-century L.A.: both the multitudinous roar of life and the untenable, unconscionable inequality."

—Steph Cha, winner of the Los Angeles Times
Book Prize for *Your House Will Pay*

"Baldwin's outsider status gives him a perfect vantage point to challenge, embrace or confront what it means to live in LA in the twenty-first century . . . LA is presented as a place that challenges preconceptions, an endless horizon of possibilities where you're meant to make your own narrative and find your own self, in amongst a crowd of others seeking to do exactly the same thing. This episodic piece of narrative non-fiction sub-divides the urban experience into personal vignettes, filtered through the city's copious literature and the many voices Baldwin meets on his quest to understand LA. It's a book about planning as much as people, and why LA is so utterly resistant to the latter whilst also being such a neophiliac's paradise."

—*Wallpaper**

Vincent Perini

Rosecrans Baldwin

Everything NOW

Rosecrans Baldwin is the author of *The Last Kid Left*, *You Lost Me There*, and *Paris, I Love You but You're Bringing Me Down*. He is a frequent contributor to *GQ* and a cofounder of the online zine *The Morning News*. He lives in Los Angeles.

Everything NOW

LESSONS FROM THE CITY-STATE OF LOS ANGELES

Everything NOW

Rosecrans Baldwin

 MCD PICADOR FARRAR, STRAUS AND GIROUX NEW YORK

MCD
Picador
120 Broadway, New York 10271

Some of these chapters previously appeared, in substantially different form, in the following publications: *Gen* (Medium.com) ("Risk a Lot, Win a Little"); *GQ* ("Anything Can Happen at Any Second," "To Be a Somebody Without a Something Is to Be a Nobody," "Some Are Footloose, Some Are Barnacles," "What Happens Next Door Happens in Madagascar"); and *Mental Floss* ("There's Nothing to See Here, and That's the Point").

Grateful acknowledgment is made for permission to reproduce material from the diaries and journals of Octavia E. Butler. Copyright © by Octavia E. Butler. Reprinted by permission of Writers House LLC acting as agent for the Estate.

Frontmatter map by June Park.

The Library of Congress has cataloged the MCD hardcover edition as follows:
Names: Baldwin, Rosecrans, author.
Title: Everything now : lessons from the city-state of Los Angeles / Rosecrans Baldwin.
Other titles: Lessons from the city-state of Los Angeles
Description: First edition. | New York : MCD / Farrar, Straus and Giroux, 2021.
Identifiers: LCCN 2020058359 | ISBN 9780374150426 (hardcover) Subjects: LCSH: Los Angeles (Calif.)—Civilization. | Los Angeles (Calif.)—Social conditions. | Interviews—California—Los Angeles Region. | Los Angeles (Calif.)—Description and travel. | City-states—United States.
Classification: LCC F869.L85 B35 2021 | DDC 979.4/94—dc23
LC record available at https://lccn.loc.gov/2020058359

Paperback ISBN: 978-1-250-84919-9

Designed by Abby Kagan

Our books may be purchased in bulk for promotional, educational, or business use. Please contact your local bookseller or the Macmillan Corporate and Premium Sales Department at 1-800-221-7945, extension 5442, or by email at MacmillanSpecialMarkets@macmillan.com.

Picador® is a U.S. registered trademark and is used by Macmillan Publishing Group, LLC, under license from Pan Books Limited.

For book club information, please visit facebook.com/picadorbookclub or email marketing@picadorusa.com.

mcdbooks.com • Follow us on Twitter, Facebook, and Instagram at @mcdbooks
picadorusa.com • Instagram: @picador • Twitter and Facebook: @picadorusa

10 9 8 7 6 5 4 3 2 1

To R.K.

In any random, sprawling, decomposing thing
is the charming string
of its history—and what it will be next.

—from "Distance and a Certain Light," by May Swenson

CONTENTS

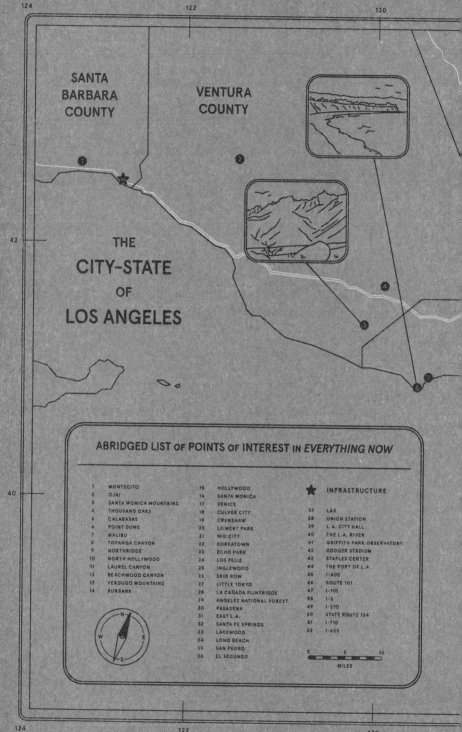

SANTA
BARBARA
COUNTY

VENTURA
COUNTY

THE
CITY-STATE
OF
LOS ANGELES

ABRIDGED LIST OF POINTS OF INTEREST IN *EVERYTHING NOW*

1	MONTECITO	15	HOLLYWOOD	★ INFRASTRUCTURE
2	OJAI	16	SANTA MONICA	
3	SANTA MONICA MOUNTAINS	17	VENICE	
4	THOUSAND OAKS	18	CULVER CITY	37 LAX
5	CALABASAS	19	CRENSHAW	38 UNION STATION
6	POINT DUME	20	LEIMERT PARK	39 L.A. CITY HALL
7	MALIBU	21	MID CITY	40 THE L.A. RIVER
8	TOPANGA CANYON	22	KOREATOWN	41 GRIFFITH PARK OBSERVATORY
9	NORTHRIDGE	23	ECHO PARK	42 DODGER STADIUM
10	NORTH HOLLYWOOD	24	LOS FELIZ	43 STAPLES CENTER
11	LAUREL CANYON	25	INGLEWOOD	44 THE PORT OF L.A.
12	BEACHWOOD CANYON	26	SKID ROW	45 I-405
13	VERDUGO MOUNTAINS	27	LITTLE TOKYO	46 ROUTE 101
14	BURBANK	28	LA CAÑADA FLINTRIDGE	47 I-110
		29	ANGELES NATIONAL FOREST	48 I-5
		30	PASADENA	49 I-210
		31	EAST L.A.	50 STATE ROUTE 134
		32	SANTA FE SPRINGS	51 I-710
		33	LAKEWOOD	52 I-605
		34	LONG BEACH	
		35	SAN PEDRO	
		36	EL SEGUNDO	

0   5   10
MILES

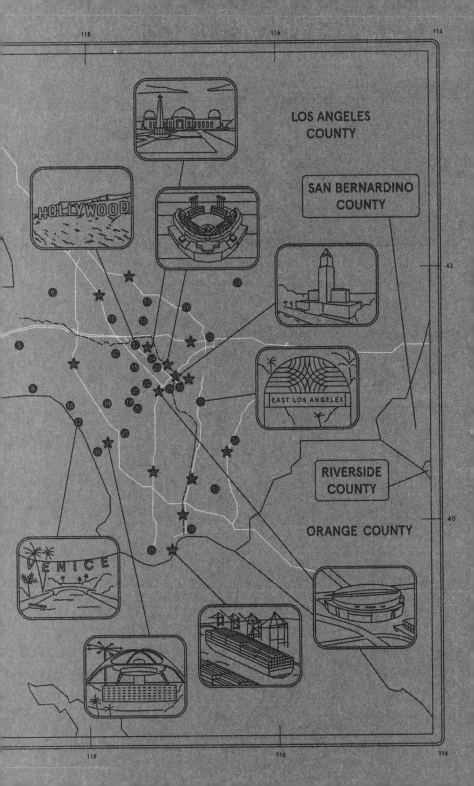

LOS ANGELES
COUNTY

SAN BERNARDINO
COUNTY

HOLLYWOOD

EAST LOS ANGELES

RIVERSIDE
COUNTY

ORANGE COUNTY

VENICE

118   116   114

42

40

Anything Can Happen at Any Second

The United States of Los Angeles • Interpreting "L.A." • Crucible of a culture • Revenge City: The Phantom Cyclist • A placeless place • City-states of the future • The five little kings (of metaphor) • Where does the garbage go?

1.0 Los Angeles, California, is enormously ambiguous. It is ambiguously enormous. Almost ninety separate villages of more than ten million people, spread across more than forty-five hundred square miles of swampland glazed by cement, mountains and canyons abutting an ocean, desert parcels cracked by quakes. It is bigger than forty American states in population. Bigger economically than nearly all of them, not to mention Saudi Arabia, Norway, or Taiwan. Nearly a quarter of the way into the twenty-first century, Los Angeles had straggled, sprawled, and germinated to become a swamp-thing megalopolis, so boundless it was nearly impossible to perceive head-on.

Less of a city than a county.

Less of a community than a climate.

Less of a metropolis than an eighty-eight-city nation-state.

1.1 In fact, Los Angeles is the largest government entity in the United States that is not a state, but to say so requires a definition of what's meant anytime "Los Angeles" is invoked by locals: Metropolitan Los Angeles, El Lay, or the Southland. Not the city in name but the place in realness. Because no one in Greater Los Angeles hears the name "L.A." and pictures only Boyle Heights, Downtown, or Venice without also thinking of Beverly Hills, Compton, and Hollywood.

Roving micheladas in the San Pedro Fish Market.

Roaming offering plates in Korean churches in the San Fernando Valley.

Santa Clarita, San Bernardino, San Clemente.

Definitely no one brings to mind the Los Angeles of authorized cartography, drawn by centuries of conquest and boom, that looks on maps less like the principal metropolis of the Western United States than a palm tree blown west by heavy winds.

1.2   Conceptually, Los Angeles is unequaled. The most populous county in the most populous state, it is the United States' seat of destitution and gated communities. Capital of incarceration and liberal policies. Recently, L.A.'s economy outperformed Chicago and New York. Joel Garreau, writing in *Edge City* in 1991—"Every single American city that is growing, is growing in the fashion of Los Angeles, with multiple urban cores"—sounded like a descendent of J. Torrey Connor and her *Saunterings in Summerland* from 1902: "A bustling, wide-awake metropolis has pushed north, east, south and west—over the hills where the vaquero tended his herds; over the gravel flats where stood the shack of the Digger; straight across the broad acres of the rancho, obliterating the last trace of the land baron's hacienda."

The face of America's housing crisis, a poster child for American hunger, a research experiment into income inequality gone horribly wrong—L.A. is both megacity and suburb, multicentered and scattered. As of the 2010 census, it was the most densely populated urbanized area in the United States. In the words of locally born Héctor Tobar, the Pulitzer Prize–winning journalist and author, Los Angeles seems to appear to the twenty-first century what New York City had been to its forerunner, "the crucible where a new national culture is being molded, where its permutations and contradictions can be seen most clearly."

1.3 One morning in 2014, a few weeks after my wife, Rachel, and I moved to Los Angeles, a large white man pedaled up to me on a bicycle and skidded to a halt. He was sunburned, covered in grime. His bike was sized for a ten-year-old boy; perhaps it had recently belonged to a ten-year-old boy. The man said in a low voice, "If I made a movie called *Revenge City*, would you go watch it?"

"I'm sorry?"

"If I made a movie, *Revenge City*, would you watch it?"

I didn't know what to say. "Based on the title, probably."

"That's what I thought," he said smugly, and pedaled away.

1.4 The book in your hands, in your ears, as you ride the bus or sit in your den with a cup of tea or something stronger—ideally, whatever circumstances make reading more pleasant for you—is an assessment, after several years of interviews and reporting, of the relationship between Los Angeles and its citizens, with an aim to demonstrate that the standard way of thinking about these people and their society often rests on a misunderstanding, that L.A. is just another big city in the United States, when actually it is something else.

Los Angeles has long resisted classification. People often struggle to describe it. "Old town, lost town, shabby town, crook town" (Raymond Chandler, *The High Window*, 1942). "I often tell people that Los Angeles makes no sense if you talk about it out loud: the land of slow-float car chases and girls with Mercurochrome hair" (Lynell George, "Native to the Place," 2001). For my part, it is the only place in the United States where I can stand anywhere and feel like I am in the middle of everything, and also like I am nowhere at all. Joan Didion said of Los Angeles, in an interview in 1973, "Every minute is a tabula rasa. There it is—by itself—no back or forward references. Just Right Now."

Crucible city. Edge city. Revenge city. To attempt to say what is Los Angeles, other than "by itself," sometimes feels like trying to pin down a cloud. The "itself" part is difficult to account for, too.

1.5 But what is it? A 2010 article in *Forbes* magazine by Joel Kotkin said that the concept of a "city-state" was making a comeback. "Athens, Carthage or Venice may have constituted the great city-states of the past, but the 21st century is likely to create its own batch of luxuriant successors." Ten years later, a piece in *Le Monde diplomatique*, published in the throat of a global coronavirus pandemic, suggested the same thing. "Many city decision-makers feel national governments are too bogged down in ideological and partisan conflicts to act effectively," Benoît Bréville wrote, "and believe cities must come together to make up for their deficiencies."

A city-state, loosely defined, is a sovereign place composed of a metropolis and its surrounding territories. Sparta of ancient history, Singapore today. Prior to the modern rise of nation-states, the city-state model enabled civilization to flourish: Alexandria, Florence, the mueang of Southeast Asia. More recently, in addition to Singapore, Monaco and Vatican City formally qualified, and perhaps San Marino, but the *Forbes* story suggested that if criteria were redrawn to be more contemporary, more places might be eligible for possessing a list of key features: vast wealth, a large port, money laundering, international museums worth visiting, guests from overseas who bank money in local investments, efficient authoritarian order, multiple languages spoken in good restaurants serving alcohol, and an ambition to host the World Cup.

The *Forbes* article caught my eye because present-day Los Angeles felt strangely nationlike to me from the moment I arrived, and it met the writer's criteria with abundance. Great treasure was buried across its limitlessness. Non-English speakers thrived. In terms of ports, according to a 2019 report in *Bloomberg News*, L.A. maintained "a near impregnable share" of U.S. shipping. For illegal cash flow, in 2014, Assistant U.S. Attorney Robert E. Dugdale called L.A. the epicenter of narco-dollar money laundering; during the COVID-19 pandemic, federal agents seized more than $1 million after the lockdown disrupted systems used by drug trafficking groups. Meanwhile, whole swaths of the city were owned, for all intents and purposes, by moneys from Asia, Russia, and the Middle East. L.A.'s museums had become some of the world's finest, same for its restaurants, and there was no shortage of booze, or even cannabis. Finally, Los Angeles was scheduled to be one of several cities in North America to feature World Cup matches in 2026, and then the Olympics would arrive, making L.A. the first American city to host the summer games three times.

Local aesthetics also suggest an updated medieval landscape: privatized neighborhoods bristling with security features; a massive gap in richness between the gentry in their towers (the hills) and the peasants in the fields (the flatlands). In *Los Angeles: The Architecture of Four Ecologies* (1971), Reyner Banham coined the phrase "the higher the ground the higher the income," and it has remained ever true—and all of it so inconveniently disorganized, so miscellaneous, just so much weirder than other U.S. cities.

City of oddballs. City of dreams. City of loot.

Plus, L.A. remains a freak in the United States. It shares little of the bedrock Americana that anchor cities such as Chicago, New York, or Boston. It is a metropolis that doesn't adhere to its greater state in the way that cities like Houston and Austin, say, serve the Republic of Texas. Miami has its ties to Latin America, Seattle its connections to Canada and the Asian Rim, but Los Angeles's international credentials encompass the globe. The great L.A. chronicler Carey McWilliams, echoing the novelist Helen Hunt Jackson, once called Los Angeles "an island on the land," as if it were drifting away from its national moorings, and that was in the 1940s.

Perhaps the only thing still needed for Los Angeles to be a city-state, I started to think, was a sense of efficient order—though maybe ours, influenced by a mix of powers, from county officials to city politicians to eccentric billionaires, is an even newer form, not so much imposed as improvised.

1.6 If Los Angeles were a city-state, "you wouldn't want to attempt to prove it formally," Geoff Manaugh, the futurist and architectural writer, told me. He pointed out one problem:

the concept of a city-state implies a core and a periphery, and L.A. has multiple cores and is all periphery. Several academics explained how Los Angeles—so massive, so diverse—had a way of defying single stories. The author and commentator Roxane Gay, a recent local homeowner, suggested that to call present-day Los Angeles a city-state probably jumped the gun, though "at times it feels like it may actually come to that," she said. "There are so many communities that consider themselves part of L.A., and that are part of L.A." Some people suggested that L.A. County history was mostly just the story of a farm town, cow town, and boomtown rolled into one. Besides, people said, the county had always felt stateless, but was that so unique on the United States' western flank? "From the beginning, L.A. emerged as a series of small, self-contained economic units, with housing, employment, and shopping in close proximity. More than most metropolitan areas, the region still functions this way," noted a 2001 report by the Southern California Studies Center and the Brookings Institution Center on Urban and Metropolitan Policy. David L. Ulin, former book editor of the *Los Angeles Times*,* wrote in his introduction to *Another City*, an anthology of writing about Los Angeles, "When it comes to L.A., even to think about an all-out encompassing narrative is to miss the point of the place, which sprawls and tumbles shapeless like a vast amoebic mass."

Sprawlscape. Oilscape. Factoryscape.

Mike Davis, author of the L.A. history *City of Quartz*, among other books, said that in terms of money, a city-state model didn't apply: Los Angeles's economy had long been controlled by powers out of state. "Economically it

---

* Hereafter referred to as "the newspaper."

doesn't conform to the classical city-state because it's not self-sustaining," he told me. Though it wasn't wrong at all, Davis thought, to approach a city-state as a metaphor for L.A., particularly because the government of the county was so unique. Los Angeles County, the largest local governmental unit in North America, was overseen by an elected panel of five supervisors—the "five little kings," Davis called them—each representing more than two million people, with immense administrative, legislative, even judicial powers. Also, the county sheriff ran the world's largest sheriff's department and the largest jail system in the United States, basically reporting to nobody save the voters, and then only on occasion. "It's just an immensely powerful, largely secret government," Davis said.

When we got off the phone, I underlined in my notes, "as a metaphor."

Metaphor: a figure of speech offering one thing for another.

A stand-in. A stuntman. A body double.

1.7 For several years, the only other thing I knew for certain about Los Angeles was something I felt shortly after arriving: that anything could happen at any second, which provoked in me a sense of doom or wild hope, depending on the day. I note this because, like a lot of my reactions to Los Angeles, it was confusing, but that puzzlement gradually became a plan—to look at the county up close. Read the books, drive the miles, meet the people, see if I might de Tocqueville my way around and test whether a metaphor could address the questions in my head.

So, a city-state. Where were the borders? Who were the kings? Where did their consigliere sleep, who were their jesters, and who kept the keys to the front gate?

Where did the garbage go?

What did the people believe?

As to how far any efforts in this book agree with those of others, the author does not care much; what I've written makes little claim to novelty beyond the nature of details people shared with me. And let's get this out of the way: I have no innate credibility to write about Los Angeles. My nearest connection is William Starke Rosecrans, an ancestor who served as a Union general in the Civil War, bought land afterward near San Pedro, and was elected U.S. representative from California's First District. Rosecrans Avenue, running through southern L.A., is named after him, just like me. But I come from Illinois, Tennessee, and Connecticut. I studied in rural Maine and urban South Africa. Before Los Angeles, Rachel and I lived in New York City; Paris, France; and the woods of North Carolina. All of which is to say that I'm a little indifferent as to whether what I put down here has been thought by somebody before me, because it seems so likely; if anything, the deeper my research and reporting went, the greater my appreciation grew for others' confessions. "I don't want to live here, but a stay here rather amuses me. It's a sort of crazy-sensible," D. H. Lawrence once wrote in a letter. "Pero speaking from the heart . . . right here, right now estoy en el cielo. Y ¿sabes que? Aqui me quedo, for now" (Susana Chávez-Silverman, *Scenes from la Cuenca de Los Angeles y otros Natural Disasters*). As Douglas Suisman said in *Los Angeles Boulevard: Eight X-Rays of the Body Public* (1989), "I soon found myself obsessed by L.A.'s great riddle: can a city be a city without appearing to be one?"

Questions abound. Why do conversations in Los Angeles tend to feel more wide-open? Why is the mood often sublimely tense? Why does it feel like history is happening all at once?

For the brief period we were here, how had we known ourselves to be?

How did it feel to be us?

LESSON 2

To Be a Somebody Without a Something Is to Be a Nobody

Self-improvement through hysteria • A city-state of incubators • Remarketing a "cure" • Octavia E. Butler • Common personality types found in Los Angeles County • The Western concept of self-willing • Loneliness, a historical account • Urban planning from the Book of Isaiah • Erotic court photography • The business of enrollment • Psychotic breaks • Beatniks, Buddhists, Birchers • Al Green is good • "A radio imagination"

2.0 In a darkened underground room near the airport, I yelled things at my father I wouldn't say to him at gunpoint. My mother heard stuff even worse. My parents sat across from me, holding hands, while roughly a hundred and fifty people shouted at their own families. Entrepreneurs and actors. Executives and nurse technicians. Latino, white, Asian, Black. Every twenty seconds or so, the noise got louder, when on top of it came the sound of the leader, our "trainer," a fifty-something white woman with an emotional choke hold on her voice, who shouted into her handheld microphone as if our lives hung in the balance, *What did they do to you? Tell them what they did!*

The room was a circus of tortured beasts.

I hate you, you fucking asshole!

Why couldn't you love meeeeeeeeee?!??!

AiaiaiiaiaAIIAGHHGHGHGHGHGaiiaiaiaAGH-GHGH

Call it hysterical transference. Call it psychological strip-mining. Not a single parent spoke, because they were only there in spirit: we had projected their likenesses onto our "dyad" partner, the person sitting across from us in the mayhem, knees clasping knees, another traumatized man or woman likewise yelling stuff, and the fantasy worked—I really did see my parents, staring back at me with shattered looks. Though by that point I was mentally crooked from emotional manipulation and little sleep, all part of a five-day "training" hosted by Mastery in Transformational Training (M.I.T.T.), stage one in a three-tier curriculum in which I'd been doing this kind of stuff for several days, late into the night, less than a mile from Los Angeles International Airport (LAX) in a high-pressure underground setting, a room where the rules about what I could and could not do were strictly enforced. Like when I should urinate or defecate, when I could speak to other people, when I was permitted to drink water or eat food.

Then our trainer told us to picture our parents dead. Which may not sound like a big deal, but we'd been messed with for several days straight. Hell broke loose. Howling. Roaring. Call it mass abreaction. I started sobbing, to a point where I was bent double, head between my legs, feeling like I was about to vomit on my partner's shoes.

In a moment of lucidity, I thought to myself, while a Black woman near me crumpled to her knees, *This really isn't how this was supposed to go.*

M.I.T.T. was a self-help program based in Culver City, a portion of the city-state best known for film and television production. The program did not market itself as a piece of entertainment. According to its website, M.I.T.T. offered "an action-oriented, experiential learning program that addresses all dimensions of human nature." Beginners were encouraged to start with their "Basic Training," a five-day class that cost about $700 and would enable "discovery in the most crucial aspects of your life." Beyond that, the website was vague about what happened in the training.

Months earlier, a woman named Sonja had been bursting to tell me about a "transformation workshop" she attended that changed her life. She refused to explain how it worked exactly, saying that people needed to experience it for themselves. A telephone interview was required to enroll. It involved questions about my mental health. "Have you ever tried to commit suicide?" "Have you ever been in a coma?" "Do you acknowledge that no one at M.I.T.T. is a trained mental-health professional?"

I said, "Really?"

It started to feel like upselling. The woman explained how the Basic Training was only step one in a three-part program, and students really needed to sign up for their Advanced Training ($1,195) and Legacy Program ($1,595) to see maximum results. "The training will have you question your beliefs," she said. "It's going to be uncomfortable. Can I count on you to participate?"

"Can you be more specific?"

"Can I count on you to participate?"

"But in what?"

She sighed with frustration. "You get to have catharsis."

"Catharsis?"

"I don't want to give you everything before you experience it."

On a Wednesday evening, about 150 "trainees" entered a hotel ballroom to the sounds of Tracy Chapman's song "Change." We were every color, all ages, as diverse as L.A. County. As we arrived, a bunch of M.I.T.T. veterans, equally diverse though dressed in formal wear, applauded us wildly with big smiles on their faces. Rows of chairs faced an empty stage. A pair of women shouted, "FILL UP THE FRONT ROWS FIRST." Finally, the doors were closed and the trainer took the stage, a woman I'll call Aunt Lydia, who told us she'd been doing these workshops around the world for thirty years. "Trust me," Aunt Lydia said, laughing, getting comfortable, "you have no idea what you're getting into."

Aunt Lydia continued to speak, often digressing, for about two hours, which is perhaps best reduced to a question-and-answer format. *What did she say?* That by enrolling in M.I.T.T., we'd entered a three-stage curriculum that would last about four months, from Basic to Advanced to Legacy—or "LP"—their combined purpose being to show us how to live a life of no regrets, discover our most authentic self, and become clear about our purpose in life. *But how exactly?* By experiencing a number of "breakthroughs," achievable with M.I.T.T.'s proprietary "technology." *Like one of those E-Meters the Scientologists use?* No. *Doesn't technology need to have some scientific backing?* According to Aunt Lydia, we should trust the process because the technology was profound and had worked for hundreds of thousands of people before us. *So where is this technology obtainable?* Primarily around Los Angeles, mostly in the Advanced and Legacy courses, though a taste would be obtained during these five days of Basic. Also, the Advanced Training, assuming we wanted to continue—and we definitely, definitely would, Aunt Lydia said—would start a week after our Basic was complete. "The training was designed, and it *was* designed, many, many years ago," Aunt Lydia said, though she didn't seem to know who created it. ("Who in hell designed this?" she exclaimed at one point.) Nevertheless, "this has been working for over forty years," producing results "so priceless, so profound, they'd never have happened otherwise." Saying this made Aunt Lydia frown, choke up, and start to cry. A man sitting next to me sniffled in response, as if by reflex. *If you had to estimate how many times Aunt Lydia choked up and nearly* cried per day, causing other people around the room to choke up and nearly cry or begin crying? One dozen times? *So what was the subtext of the whole thing?* "The training is a profound opportunity," Aunt Lydia said. After all, who wanted to live a life of regrets? At one point she invoked Henry David Thoreau as her inspiration—whose last words, she said, were "no regrets"—while over and over she insisted how valuable the technology was, how life-changing the training would be, that if our sunburnt minds weren't completely blown away—*Doth the lady protest too much?* Well, yeah.

According to *Thoreau, The Poet-Naturalist: With Memorial Verses*, a biography from 1873 by Thoreau's friend William Ellery Channing, his last intelligible words were "moose" and "Indian."

Around the two-hour mark I needed to use the restroom and walked discreetly to the exit. Aunt Lydia, explaining that we needed to approach the training as if our lives depended on it, said loudly, with heavy sarcasm, "Or you can get up and leave and go to the bathroom." The crowd laughed, swiveling. Staff members stared with alarm. I kept going toward the doors while two of them moved toward me, such that I had to awkwardly squeeze between them to leave.

When I returned, Aunt Lydia was asking people to suggest ways we could avoid participating in the training. "Being late." "Being distracted." She noticed me and said to a volunteer, "Add to the list: going to the bathroom." She turned to the crowd and said angrily, "The doors are open, okay? But notice, if you leave the room, you're making space for other people to leave the room." This made her choke up and wipe her eye. "And that's someone whose life is at stake. And you're . . . you're . . . you're walking away," she said, her voice faltering.

Suggesting that by going to the restroom, I'd nearly ruined someone's life.

A search on the internet for "cults" in Los Angeles around that period showed M.I.T.T. ranking fourth, behind several megachurches. As one person commented online about M.I.T.T., "When more than one review for a 'business' starts with 'This is seriously NOT a cult!!' you should probably avoid that place."

2.1 By 2021, Los Angeles contained around eleven million people. In terms of population, just "the Valley," the San Fernando Valley, was among the ten largest cities in the United States. The people of L.A. spanned the world's variety, in slices named Little Ethiopia, Historic Filipinotown, Tehrangeles. It was estimated that nearly two hundred languages were used in homes; in the public schools, ninety-plus. The volunteers office at LAX sent me a chart demonstrating forty languages on offer in their information booths, including speakers in Thai (six), Indonesian (five), Polish (four), Turkish (three), Hakka (two), and Gujarati (one). "We have these little nation-states all over," said Martin Zogg, executive director at the International Rescue Committee in Los Angeles. "If you go to Westminster, Garden Grove, Fountain Valley, you see the Vietnamese nation-state. If you go to East Long Beach, you see the Cambodian/Pacific Islander nation-state. You come to Glendale, you see the Armenian nation-state. The west side, the Persian nation-state."

Los Angeles had long welcomed refugees, Zogg said, but that didn't make it any easier for them to adjust to living here. L.A. was already tough for newcomers to grasp—the scale and geography, or just how to get around—and refugees often had it harder. "Add on being persecuted for years on end, going through the resettlement process, landing here perhaps without any support—it's triply hard."

People often thought of nationhood as the inevitable stopping point for human communities, a zenith that societies simply reached. But countries had only divvied the globe for the past three centuries or so. For the so-called Western world, political scientists point to the treaties of Westphalia, signed in 1648, as a pivot toward today's international system. Whereas, for much longer before that, humans had organized themselves into smaller units through empires and dynasties—societies with their own rules, customs, common feelings.

Self-governing, self-celebrating, self-fashioned.

Among L.A.'s millions, in addition to refugees, there were strata common and uncommon: construction workers, investment bankers, and the idle wealthy; the working poor, the working poor who lived out of their cars, and the working poor who slept in tents. Freelance futures traders, freelance fitness trainers, cloistered Dominican nuns selling pumpkin bread from behind security gates. Right-wing television hosts. Drag queen television hosts. Early on Sunday mornings I liked to listen to an excitable Christian talkshow host in Burbank who condemned yoga as sacrilegious witchcraft.

And still, for all the variety, the city-state, built from landgrabs and straggle, had long possessed a single defining feature to describe the populace: a place for the self-made, the self-fabricated, and the self-assured, and also those who would help themselves to whatever they could seize. Such that the practice of self-help, in a hodgepodge of forms, had long felt like Los Angeles's most widespread habit, after tacos/burgers/pastrami.

But sometimes the two concepts, "self-help" and "self-made," got confused.

In 1921, John Steven McGroarty, a poet who later became a congressman, wrote, "Los Angeles is the most celebrated of all incubators of new creeds, codes of ethics, philosophies—no day passes without the birth of something of this nature never heard of before." The author Eve Babitz had her own version of this: "It's very easy to stand L.A., which is why it's almost inevitable that all sorts of ideas get entertained, to say nothing of lovers" (*Slow Days, Fast Company*).

2.2   One word that never appeared in Aunt Lydia's lectures at M.I.T.T. was *Lifespring*. Lifespring was a popular self-help program from the 1970s and '80s, similar to groups like Landmark Forum or EST. As a large-group awareness training program (LGAT), as they were known among psychologists, Lifespring had offered a five-day "Basic" training followed by an "Advanced" class, followed by a "Leadership" program, all part of a self-help curriculum.

Marc Fisher, a journalist for *The Washington Post*, attended one of Lifespring's Basic trainings in 1987. While reporting on the group, he learned that Lifespring's executives had known for years that some trainees experienced adverse reactions. The group's founder, John Hanley, told Fisher, "If a thousand people get benefit from the training, and one person is harmed, I'd can it." And yet, according to Fisher's investigation, over the years there were dozens of "casualties," Lifespring's name for people who left the training with severe psychological issues.

By the time the *Post* story went to print in October 1987, according to its reporting, about thirty-five trainees had sued Lifespring; six people had died. In one case, which Lifespring settled, a man who couldn't swim was persuaded by his trainer to dive into a river to overcome his fear and drowned. "Lifespring denied any responsibility, saying that no one forced [him] to jump in the river," Fisher wrote. "'The training doesn't cause anything,' Hanley said then. 'Life causes stuff.'" In another example cited by the *Post*, a woman had an asthma attack during a training. Trainers told her the asthma was self-induced. "When she finally left the room, she wandered into a parking lot, collapsed and died after five days in a coma." Lifespring denied responsibility and paid the woman's family $450,000 to settle their claim.

Thanks to Lifespring's success, Hanley became a multimillionaire. Previous to Lifespring, he had committed a felony, Fisher learned. In 1969 Hanley and a partner were found guilty of mail fraud. In a separate case, the Wisconsin Justice Department sued Hanley and others for running a pyramid scheme, unrelated to Lifespring, which he paid to settle in 1973. Hanley denied responsibility and only paid up, he told the *Post*, because he didn't want to pay a lawyer.

Fast-forward to 1998. A Dutch woman named Margo Majdi, a Lifespring trainee and the owner of a beauty salon in Beverly Hills, purchased the rights to the trainings from Hanley. After a publicist told her that Lifespring had gained a bad reputation and she should consider rebranding, Majdi renamed it, coming up with M.I.T.T. "When I made it Mastery in Transformational Training, everybody thought I was crazy," she told me later during an interview at her home. "Notice now everything is called mastery, mastermind, master this, master tribe . . ."

The second half of my first evening with M.I.T.T. continued after a short break. Aunt Lydia made us promise to be
back in our seats "by the time the music stops." About twenty
minutes later, the music—once again, Tracy Chapman—
shifted loudly to Richard Strauss's "Also sprach Zarathustra,"
known as the theme from *2001: A Space Odyssey*. People
ran to their chairs. During the final notes, Aunt Lydia strode
to the stage. A dozen people were still walking in when the
music finished. She commanded them to stop. "Do you acknowledge you broke your promise?"

They stared in confusion.

"Do you acknowledge you broke your promise?" she repeated, more sinister.

For the next hour Aunt Lydia explained a set of "ground
rules" we'd need to obey through the remainder of the
training. No tardiness. No phones. No "side talking" with
others, which meant no conversing unless instructed. No
saying "bless you" if someone sneezed. Also, no alcohol or
drugs, and no eating or drinking at any time in the ballroom. People raised their hands; several wanted to be able
to sip water for medical reasons. Aunt Lydia confronted
them individually. By the time a third and fourth person explained what sounded like a pretty valid medical reason for
needing to drink water—an older couple with respiratory
issues, for example—she seemed appalled. She turned to
us, sneering. "I've honestly never had this happen before in
a training." When another person said she was on a special
diet that required her to eat at precise times, Aunt Lydia
started laughing and looked at us like, *Who does she think
she is?* The woman said she merely wanted to know when
breaks would be scheduled so she could plan out her meals.

"I won't tell you that," Aunt Lydia said. "No one here will tell you that."

Around midnight we split into smaller groups, each with a "small-group leader"—all of them there as volunteers, I later learned—who established times we would be required to telephone the next morning to check in. I got home an hour later and fell asleep around two; my alarm went off at five for work. At the appointed check-in time of 7:30 a.m., I called Jon, my small-group leader. He asked how my first day had gone. I wanted to tell him I couldn't believe people paid good money for such crap. I said something about how it seemed like Therapy 101 with a side order of humiliation. Also, if the training was good enough to be "technology," why was it kept a secret—in the city of self-promotion no less? Who invented it anyway?

Instead of responding to my questions, Jon asked, "So where do you think these feelings came from?" I said defensively, Probably my hatred of bullies? Jon said, "Well . . . ," then thanked me for my honesty, which he said was integral to any M.I.T.T. journey, and he looked forward to seeing me that night.

(M.I.T.T. declined to confirm or comment on specific exercises and interactions. Aunt Lydia, the instructor, said, "The training processes are confidential, simply for the purpose of spontaneity for the participants. Otherwise it is like a spoiler for a movie. It renders the exercise useless.")

On the second night in the basement, the subject was victimization: realizing how, why, and when we'd been victims in our lives and who had victimized us. But the lesson came with M.I.T.T.'s special spin, straight from Lifespring, that victimhood was mostly self-made, and a person needed to find a way to take personal responsibility for whatever had happened to them in order to overcome it. But mostly day two was about the ground rules again. (Beginning on the second day of the training, taking notes or using phones in the ballroom was forbidden, so any quotations or exercises described here are based on recollections recorded in memos and notes made during breaks and after sessions, and confirmed by other attendants.) After one break, to the bellowing strains of *2001*, several people returned late, and Aunt Lydia read them the riot act. She singled out a woman I'll call Nadia.

You, the one twirling your hair. That's some kind of survival tic you've picked up?

Sure, that's it, Nadia said dryly.

Do you have a problem with me? Aunt Lydia asked.

I think you're obnoxious.

Oh, you do.

Yes, I do.

Nadia had an accent, maybe British. Aunt Lydia started to imitate it—she often did this; she seemed to find it hilarious—while accusing Nadia of needing to be right. Nadia accused her of the same. The argument went on for two minutes while people in the audience squirmed, until a baffled Aunt Lydia gave Nadia the finger. Nadia gave her the finger right back. Toward the conclusion of their fight Aunt Lydia yelled at us, *How many of you think I'm a badass amazing super coach?* Most hands went up. *And how many of you think I'm some kind of obnoxious bitch?* About twenty people, including me.

A source later confirmed that Nadia continued with M.I.T.T. after the Basic training and ultimately completed the LP program.

Beyond the Advanced and LP courses, M.I.T.T. also offered a "Ph.D. program," with no actual academic accreditation, plus workshops, retreats, and corporate trainings conducted around Greater L.A. During my drive home late that night in the misty black, cruising north on empty freeways, the main purpose of M.I.T.T. seemed pretty clear to me: to make Ms. Majdi, Aunt Lydia, and whoever else a bunch of money, in a system where the biggest epiphanies were still one course away. And surely, even more faucets of cash would be opened if they persuaded us to draft our friends and family to join. Multiple people informed me that close to 100 percent of trainees were referrals—M.I.T.T. didn't advertise—in part because students were eventually expected to recruit, or "enroll," outsiders.

On day three, the world outside the basement would be unknown to us while we focused inward. In one exercise, performed in the dark, we knelt on the ground while visualizing ourselves digging through a junkyard. The "garbage" around us was broken promises: those made to us by our family and friends; those we'd made ourselves and not lived up to. Meanwhile, the staff blasted us with songs by Cat Stevens and Whitney Houston to rock us weepy— they did this at loud volume to stoke our emotions—and on top of it all, Aunt Lydia would shout, *Who promised to love you? Who promised to keep you safe? Maybe you were abused as a child! Maybe you were sexually abused! Who broke their promise to you? Keep digging!* Slowly but surely, young women bawled, old men sobbed and rocked, a personal trainer pounded the floor with his fists. I'd made the mistake of kneeling about six feet in front of Aunt Lydia, so anytime she yelled into the microphone, it almost split my ears, though I also heard her, mid–choke up, put down the microphone at one point and chastise a staff member in a normal tone, some problem with the soundtrack; then she picked up the mic again and resumed her trembling, vulnerable voice.

It wasn't until a few days after my time in M.I.T.T. that I discovered *The Washington Post*'s reporting about Lifespring. So much was familiar: the humiliation of trainees; the hokey fantasies and weeping participants; an impression that the "technology," once peeked at behind the curtain, appeared to drain wallets by fiddling with exhausted minds. According to the article, Hanley, Lifespring's founder, got a D in the only psychology class he ever took. Even the story's title rang a bell: "I Cried Enough to Fill a Glass."

Marc Fisher was now a senior editor at the paper. "This is the perfect time for a resurgence of interest in these kinds of programs," he said. "We're living in a time that's tailor-made for an M.I.T.T., a Lifespring, or an EST. It's a time of tremendous dislocation in people's careers and the economies of families. It's a time of political polarization. It's a time of loss of community as a result of social media. It's only natural that people are craving the connections and the meaning that these programs promise." I asked him what stood out in his memory from thirty years ago. "The relative ease with which the guy running the program could assert control over a large room of people. And not just the willingness but the eagerness of people to be led and for someone to take authority over them." He added, "Anytime we're in a crisis of government, or parenting, or family structure—all those things that made this society so unsettled—for somebody to come along and tell you, 'This is how things are going to be. This is what you need to do

to fix it. And then everything's going to be okay, or better'—
that's pretty powerful."

At the end of day three, in semi-darkness, we sat in
silence. The doors weren't locked, but it felt as if they were.
Everyone bowed their heads while volunteers blasted us with
Tracy Chapman's "The Rape of the World" and Aunt Lydia
read aloud statistics about global suffering, the amount of
pollution caused by single-use plastics, how many shelter
dogs were euthanized each year, something about how many
dogs got eaten by Chinese people. By that point she had told
us several times that she ran a dog rescue on the side—it
seemed to explain the preponderance of canine-related statistics. Anyway, the world was doomed, humans were re-
pulsive, and all of us were lost, lost to ourselves, lost to the
world—a dark underground room of lost, doomed humans
crying softly.

The name "Aunt Lydia" refers to a character created
by the novelist Margaret Atwood, whose Aunt Lydia is a
woman of seeming moral perfection. For all the admon-
ishments and hubris at M.I.T.T., the sanctimony invoked
around the power of the curriculum, it felt like I'd stumbled
my way into self-help's version of *The Handmaid's Tale*.

2.3 Octavia Estelle Butler, one of the most influential writers
ever produced by the city-state, always knew where she
was, where she was going, and where she was from, even
when it pained her, especially when it pained her. "I was
born in Pasadena, California, in 1947 and except for some
scattered months of living in the desert just outside Victor-
ville, I've lived in Pasadena ever since," she once wrote in

a note. "This is a terrible thing to have done and I hope to leave soon, if only for Los Angeles."

Butler would become the award-winning, bestselling author of more than a dozen works of fiction. She was the first Black woman to break through in science fiction, the first science fiction writer of any color or gender to be awarded a MacArthur "Genius" Grant. Butler died in 2006, but her legacy has since flourished, and her archive is now part of the Huntington Library, near Pasadena, where it has become one of the most requested, one librarian said, from a collection that houses a Gutenberg Bible, the first two quartos of *Hamlet*, and the first seven drafts of *Walden* by Henry David Thoreau.

"Here we are, her spiritual children numbering in the thousands, come to claim the future," N. K. Jemisin wrote in a foreword for a recent reprinting of Butler's *Parable of the Sower*—Jemisin also being an award-winning, bestselling Black female science fiction author. The legacy of Octavia E. Butler, however, had not always been certain. At the Huntington, page after page of her journals and correspondence were filled with signs of Butler trying to forge herself into an artist. "I shall be a bestselling author," she wrote, long before she was one. "This is my life. I write bestselling novels. My novels go onto bestseller lists on or shortly after publication." Frequently, her predictions were accompanied by slightly less confident exhortations to see it through. "I will find a way to do this. So be it! See to it!"

It is not difficult to find people in Los Angeles seeking transformation, and also those who would help them. Mystics, psychics, preachers. Life coaches who advertise their services on telephone poles. In the San Fernando Valley, a man known as "The O-Man," an orgasm whisperer, was said to make women reach ecstasy dozens of times in a single session, though in the manner of a personal trainer. "I fix their posture and mobilize their joints," he said in an online interview. "It's pretty simple, just a twenty-to-thirty-minute massage followed by two hours of coming." And when each season of the future arrived, a new food fad blew through town ("any three-day cleanse for $90"), a new treatment—the "Viora Reaction," the "Vampire Facelift"—to fix what citizens might not have known was wrong about themselves, but others knew. If self-help was a habit in the United States, it seemed pathological in the city-state. For research, I hired a "people walker" to walk me around Los Feliz and discuss the news. I hired a "complexity coach" who hiked me into the mountains above Altadena while conducting talk therapy. Perhaps the discomfort underlying it all was best expressed by local resident RuPaul Charles, presenter of *RuPaul's Drag Race*, a reality competition filmed in Burbank, who closed each episode asking, "If you can't love yourself, how in the hell you gonna love somebody else?"

Butler's writings had a similar sound, at least in their undertone. Introverted, highly intelligent, an artist standing over six feet tall, Butler had been fully aware of her separateness. "I can't talk to people the way I want to," she wrote in 1964, in her late teens. "They nearly all sense a difference in me. They talk to each other, then they talk to me." From 1973: "You are nonmagnetic. Considering your solitary nature, this is good." One of the most touching notes I found was in a notebook labeled 1973–74: "Why do I do the thing opposite what I know will help me except in keeping with my personality when that opposite can cause me clear physical harm. Why do I make excellent workable plans, and then not carry them out. Why do I seem so perversely out to get myself?"

2.4 The self-made person—the artist, the athlete, the criminal— may take credit for what they make of themselves, but can also suffer the pains of the manufacturing process. And sometimes they're mistaken for a type less complete: the seeker, the addict, the traumatized.

The incomplete person, like the self-made person, is also a common L.A. type.

Occasionally they are found in the same person.

2.5 In 2016 the writer Lynell George was one of several artists commissioned by Clockshop, a local arts organization, to produce work inspired by the Butler archive to coincide with the tenth anniversary of Butler's death. "Anytime people said, 'No, you can't do that,' [Butler] suffered obviously," George said one morning in Pasadena. "When some of her relatives were telling her, 'Negro girls don't aspire to be a writer. It's okay as a hobby,' it was from every direction, and she kept pushing." George attributed Butler's will to be an artist, in part, to growing up in Pasadena, away from the East Coast's stricter traditions: "Willing yourself into being is such a western concept," George said. "That idea of, 'I'm going west, there's fewer rules there. I can do whatever.'"

George pointed out that Butler had figured out her own methods for living. She read widely, traveled, and kept up correspondence. Before a conversation she might be nervous about, Butler made notes to prepare. "She wrote out a little script of what she'd say to that person on the phone, and then she'd call up and do it. Or she's having an argument with an editor and she's written out everything she's going to say," George said. "As scared as she was about everything, she had a lot of courage."

George, also a Black female writer, born in Los Angeles, was the author of *A Handful of Earth, A Handful of Sky*, a book about Butler's process of self-making. I asked what growing up in such a place might have meant to an African American woman picturing herself as a published author someday. "From a young age, [Butler] realized, 'I don't fit in with everyone else in my little school, but I can kind of fit in in the big world,'" George said. "She knew she was different. She *knew*. She could have pressed it all down, but she didn't. She followed it. And being in a place like Los Angeles, that enabled her to find it."

In 1980, in her early thirties, Butler wrote a letter to an assistant arts editor at the newspaper. By that point she'd published several novels, including *Kindred*, which would become possibly her most popular work, in which a young Black woman is flung through time between her home in 1970s Los Angeles and a plantation in pre–Civil War Maryland. Butler's letter to her local paper, with two books enclosed, appeared to be an effort to justify why she should be reviewed. "I am a native Californian, born in Pasadena (where my second home was the public library), and living now in Los Angeles (where my second home is still the library)," she wrote. "I am the only black woman writing science fiction (there are three black men)." She would not be reviewed in the *Los Angeles Times* until 1994, more than a decade later, as far as my digging found.

Butler's voice worked itself into my skull. The further I got in the archive, the more it seemed as if, in the process of making herself, she'd needed to write self-help books to herself, for herself, just to believe the illusion, to buy the narrative. And maybe sometimes just to keep herself company. "I had to talk to myself and say: This is who you are. You are not going to change into anyone else. You've got to work with what you've got and do your best with it."

2.6 In Robert M. Fogelson's *The Fragmented Metropolis: Los Angeles, 1850–1930*, he cited an "endemic" sense of loneliness at the turn of the century, a feeling of extreme isolation. One woman commented, in 1900, "Why, I don't even know the name of my next door neighbor. I hear the water running in their bath tub as well or as better than I hear in my own tub. I know what they say and can tell you what they are doing, but I don't know what their name is and I have never cared to find out."

For more than a year I posted an ad online each month to see if anyone nearby wanted to talk about loneliness. Responses spanned the region. "It's a happening spot. So many events and wonderful things to experience—but with someone," wrote Mike from Long Beach. Jesse from Downtown said, "If you don't already have someone to go with, it's as if the events are no longer on the menu." Several people talked about the loneliness of smartphone addiction, the sense that citizens of L.A. could be transactional. "Everyone is looking for a better offer," Jason, a new resident of Sawtelle, said. "If the answer is 'You can't help me,' then there's an air of, 'I don't want to know you.'" Dekay, born in South Central, wrote, "[It is] a very detached culture. It's all about you and your own superficial bubble. People tend to be either distracted or angry. In Los Angeles, you can feel that energy. It's all superficial, a lie. People in cities don't truly know people; they are oblivious to people's emotional suffering because it hasn't touched them personally. They will only care when it deeply affects them. In the city, you are only a number. You tend to get lost in the shuffle because nobody gives a damn."

At the same time, some people were confused by the ad, thinking a query about loneliness was looking for sex, and they would proposition me—a man in North Hollywood, a couple from Bell Gardens—or ask for nude photos or send me nude photos. One man persisted in thinking he'd earn nude selfies by sharing stories of his life, though I explicitly told him this was not the case. For example, about all the people he had robbed: "Another time a guy gave me a quarter pound of weed and said pay him back later but I didn't pay him back ever," he wrote. "Another time a guy asked for an ounce so I told him it cost 300 bucks. Then I told him I had to get it first, so he gave me 300 bucks then I hopped out of his car. He texted me saying he was leaving before I could get it so when I got the weed, I didn't give him any. I've robbed 12 people. So let me see those pics."

In *On the Road*, Jack Kerouac called Los Angeles "the loneliest and most brutal of American cities." Around the same time, the English psychoanalyst Donald Winnicott, writing in *The International Journal of Psycho-Analysis*, called the capacity for a human to be alone a sophisticated phenomenon. "It is closely related to emotional maturity. The basis of the capacity to be alone is the experience of being alone in the presence of someone." During the same year that I was emailing strangers about loneliness, a group of professional video game players called the FaZe Clan, living in a mansion above Hollywood, was profiled in *The New York Times*. As a group, they were worth millions of dollars, they had millions of fans, but they talked openly about struggling with isolation, depression, days spent indoors, hidden away in bedrooms with the shades drawn. The article seemed to suggest that they couldn't have existed anywhere else but Los Angeles—yet in many ways, they didn't exist in L.A. at all. "Eventually we will all live in the internet," one said, "and I want to exist in that world."

Octavia E. Butler's father died during her childhood, and she lived much of her life with her mother. In her journals Butler often wrote about her solitude with a sense of detachment; as though solitude were a thing that didn't depend on the presence or absence of her mother or other people. In 1978, when she was thirty-one, she noted, "Strange feelings in the night. The thought that I'd better have children or I'll be alone soon. All alone. Having children is no guarantee that I won't be alone." On the same page: "There is no one— absolutely no one, no matter how enfolded and beloved— who is not lonely some of the time. All right. I am lonely, and alone too much of the time." It was the next paragraph in the journal that really cut me, to see Butler's heart and mind so conjoined: "I long to love someone. I fear to be completely alone. My mother will die and I will be completely alone. Other relatives like me. At least, none seem to dislike me. They don't love me. Why should they?"

2.7 "Woe to you who add house to house and join field to field, till no space is left and you live alone in the land" (The Book of Isaiah).

2.8 Included in the archive was one of Butler's mother's own diaries. Her entries were occasional, in a messy hand, mostly short notes about God or troubles with men. But one entry, from August 1962, was crisply legible, surrounded by empty space. "I like tennis," Butler's mother wrote, "but never had no one to play tennis with me."

About a year after I moved to Los Angeles, a friend introduced me to a man named Freddy as a potential tennis partner. Freddy liked to play early mornings before going to the office. The day we met, around seven a.m., the first thing he said was, "Come here and take a look at this. This was three hours ago." On his phone, a photograph showed him naked in a bathtub filled with milk while a woman, perched on top of him, faced the camera with an orchid protruding from her vagina. Another woman, off camera, had taken the picture, he explained. "Eventually I just had to kick them out," he said, laughing. "I hope my legs are okay to play." The orchid seemed a curious touch, I thought. The picture had needed a prop, he said, plus he liked the contrast. "Me, her, the milk, the flower."

Tennis, one of the lonelier sports, was a typical city-state pastime. All from the Los Angeles area: Jack Kramer, Stan Smith, Billie Jean King, Pete Sampras, Venus and Serena Williams. "During the tennis boom of the 1970s and '80s, all of a sudden everyone had to look like a tennis player, whether they were one or not," Randy Kramer, founder of The Racket Doctor, a popular tennis shop near Griffith Park, told me. "If you went to LAX, everybody had a tennis racquet. It was the most bizarre thing I've ever seen in my life." More recently the sport had waned globally, but county tennis courts remained busy. In Beverly Hills, a charity event held annually at a house designed by L.A. architect John Lautner featured an "infinity court," seemingly hanging off a cliff.

Born in Los Angeles, Freddy had been raised by a single father. He probably had some problems with women as a result, he confessed. At tennis, he was steady, focused by a low-simmering anger, until he started playing badly; then he'd go into a rage. Freddy made enough money as a lawyer for a nice car and a nice apartment, but the job was killing him, he said, requiring him to perform as something other than what he felt was his authentic self, the artist locked inside. "I have to be exactly what those people want. Whatever [the firm] wants, I'm like, 'Yes sir, we'll get it, we'll do it.' When I get home, I get to be myself. I get to be whoever I want."

According to recent census numbers, nearly a third of households in the city-state consisted of just one person. It explained why *House Made of Dawn*, N. Scott Momaday's 1969 Pulitzer-winning novel, still sounded fresh. "She had been in Los Angeles four years, and in all that time she had not talked to anyone. There were people all around; she knew them, worked with them—sometimes they would not leave her alone—but she did not talk to them, tell them anything that mattered in the least. She greeted them and joked with them and wished them well, and then she withdrew and lived her life. No one knew what she thought or felt or who she was."

Freddy's rage rarely left him, but he could be tender-hearted. He told me several times, defensively, worrying I had misunderstood him, that the women in his photographs were always there quite willingly. Aspiring models needed new photographs to post online, he explained, to make it seem like they were in demand, especially those just getting their start. So they reached out to him, and Freddy would make an offer: he'd shoot for free, in whatever wardrobe they liked, though in exchange he got a few nudes for his collection. Women would arrive late at night. Freddy arranged different setups, "little pools of light around the loft." First they did the photos the women wanted. "They're posing like other models pose—it's all so awkward," he told me, shaking his head. "I'm like, 'Stop trying to be sexy. Think about getting fucked.' Their eyelids start to droop, they start breathing out of their mouths. After a little while, one of them might grab my dick, then we go from there." The models and Freddy didn't always have sex, he said, but that didn't matter; the moment's purpose was transformation, of Freddy from lawyer to artist, of model from aspiring to professional, two humans lofted above the city, spotlighted for a moment, making themselves into their finer selves. "It's a process," he said contemplatively. "The journey is really amazing to watch."

I only played with Freddy a few more times. At the end of our last match, sipping water at the bench, he laughed out of the blue. "I was just thinking, the girls I was screwing when I was twenty, do you think they were banging forty-two-year-old guys on the side, too?" He laughed again, stared across the court; then his whole face fell.

I sometimes thought that Freddy was the loneliest person I'd met in Los Angeles. But that was before I joined M.I.T.T.

2.9 Shortly after my training, Margo Majdi, the founder of M.I.T.T., agreed to an interview at her home near Beverly Hills. A white SUV gleamed in the driveway. A short woman greeted me at the door in the manner of a servant and escorted me to Majdi's dining room, where we sat for an hour at a long table, surrounded by numerous mirrors. Majdi was in her mid-seventies. Her eyes were clear and tireless, and her face glowed as she spoke. Behind her, in the kitchen, a pair of chandeliers shimmered from light coming in through a window.

Majdi said she was born and raised in Holland and moved to the United States in 1970. She did Lifespring for the first time ten years later, "and it was absolutely phenomenal." Years passed while she ran her beauty salon, and in 1997 she decided to get out of the business. "I started actually working out of my house here," she said. "And I had one of my clients, she walked in, she is a doctor, and she goes, 'Oh my God, I just did Lifespring.' I go, 'Lifespring, that's still around?'"

Majdi retook the Basic Training, then jumped into the Advanced and Leadership courses, experiencing "one breakthrough after another." But the number of participants was less than half of what she remembered from 1980; recruitment had plummeted. "The business is based on enrollment," she explained. "The leadership people enroll, enroll, enroll." Majdi said that once she acquired the trainings, she didn't change much about Lifespring aside from the name. And yes, it was part of the Legacy Program, or LP, that participants were expected to recruit outsiders to M.I.T.T., but that was "to create their own legacy," she said. She declined to comment on how many people went through her trainings each month, only that numbers were up, and they did around eleven Basic Trainings a year, plus the subsequent Advanced and LP courses, not to mention all the other classes available. What did she hope newcomers would take away from the Basic Training—the one I took? "It's for them to look deeper within themselves and to really see what's stopping them," she said. "You don't know actually what you're capable of. But if you start recognizing what's stopping you, you will break through to that and actually overcome your fear, and then you might just step into the next level."

I asked her to help me understand one of Lifespring's and M.I.T.T.'s more provocative ideas, that victimhood was a choice, that a victim needed to take responsibility for whatever had happened to them. "It's like this," she said. "You know, I've been victimized in my life. You've been victimized in your life. But if I still constantly walk around being a victim, who has my power?" She added, "I'm not saying if you're raped, you're not a victim. But you know what I would say? That then again, it's how you choose to look at it. How you choose to look at everything in life. I can say, like, 'Well, you know . . .' I can say, like, 'I shouldn't have been there.'"

"That's how you take responsibility for it?" I said.

"'I shouldn't have been there,'" she intoned.

"You shouldn't have put yourself into a situation where something like rape could happen?"

"'I shouldn't have left drunk,'" she said. "'I should maybe not have been drinking that much.' 'I should have watched who I'm sitting next to.'"

"I think that's a difficult thing for people to hear," I said.

"Yes. It is."

In some of the reviews online that went negative, M.I.T.T. would be referred to as a cult, something the city-state had a rich history in fostering—the Source Family, the Manson Family, Buddhafield. Majdi laughed when I brought it up. Did I see anyone sitting on the floor, she wondered, worshipping at her feet? "The moment you came out of the womb, you're in a cult," she said. "Think about it. You're told what to say, what not to say, how to dress, how to eat." She went on to describe trainings she'd done in China, a book she published, a foundation she had started to host "transformational leadership workshops" for teenagers—painting a picture of the modern, diversified businesswoman. M.I.T.T. operated primarily around Los Angeles County, though Majdi had allowed other groups to run trainings elsewhere, she said, as long as they operated under their own names. I brought up people having unfortunate reactions to Lifespring—did M.I.T.T. ever experience anything like that? She reminded me about their screening process, keeping out applicants with troubled histories, but yes, they'd had their share of problems. "Like, I hear years later that even some people, they go, like, 'I was suicidal, Margo.' I go, 'How did you get that in my training?' But you know what? Sometimes people make up things like that. And then, so, thank God that I cannot say that anything really bad has happened. I had, actually, just a couple months ago, somebody came after us and said something bad happened. So I don't know. I don't know."

2.10 A few weeks after my training, I found a complaint from May 2017 brought against Majdi and M.I.T.T. in California's Superior Court. In the lawsuit, a woman named Dana, who took the Basic and Advanced trainings in 2015, accused M.I.T.T. of "thought reform" and "brainwashing" so intense she'd experienced a psychotic break, causing her to cycle through "extreme confabulations, violent acting out and a catatonic state requiring four-point restraint and psychiatric hospitalization."

I found Dana still living in Los Angeles. What got her into M.I.T.T. was her sister, she said, who'd been taking the LP program. At the time, Dana had been planning to hire a consultant to help her grow her photography business, but her sister convinced her that doing M.I.T.T.—the Basic Training cost about the same as the consultant—would be far more beneficial. Dana was thirty-two when she enrolled. She said that before she did the trainings, she'd never experienced anxiety. No history of addictions, eating disorders, any psychological problems. "There was absolutely no reason that I thought I would be any more at risk doing this program than anybody else," she said.

"It's a pretty nasty organization," her lawyer, Ford Greene, told me. In the past, Greene has successfully represented clients against the Church of Scientology. "The consequences on Dana were drastic and severe."

Dana described the Advanced Training as more intense than the Basic. Echoing much of what was alleged in her lawsuit, she said that in one exercise a man was persuaded to wear a diaper. She was made to walk around in a ball gown and tiara and later required to perform an exotic dance. "I think the fact that it sounds so absurd makes people not believe it. And that can be problematic, because if something sounds really outrageous, [people] very quickly will say, 'Well, that wouldn't happen to me.'" Her sister quit the LP training shortly after Dana was hospitalized. Dana recognized that her sister had been under pressure to enroll her, to fix how she was feeling, so to speak. "It's unfortunate that a group like this can take advantage of the trust you have in your family members and your friends and use that to their advantage," she said. Three years later she continued to attend a support group for cult survivors. Asked if she'd ever hired that photography consultant, she smiled ruefully and said yes. "It did wonders."

M.I.T.T. disputed Dana's allegations. Her case was dismissed owing to two arbitration agreements that Dana signed while at M.I.T.T.

In the course of my research, a connection introduced me to a young man I'll refer to as Jeremy. Mid-twenties, originally from Oregon, Jeremy learned about M.I.T.T. from a college roommate who did the trainings all the way up to the Ph.D. level and sang rapture around the experience. "I put a lot of trust in [M.I.T.T.] because he put a lot of trust in them," Jeremy said. "I didn't really know where their techniques were coming from. I didn't know if they were trained. Of course, they're not. At all." Jeremy said he'd found the Basic Training problematic but intriguing. He studied psychology in college; M.I.T.T. felt like a scam. "The moment I stepped into the first day, the first day of the Basic, the word *cult* was screaming in my head. All these people in tuxes clapping at you." He took the Advanced course after Basic but soon grew disillusioned. The exercises were a lot more negative, he said. "It was really bizarre and confusing. It was a lot more challenging to see the merits of it. It felt more like a traumatizing experience."

In his late teens, Jeremy had experienced a psychotic break, requiring a year of treatment. During the initial screening process for M.I.T.T., after he informed them about his past, he said they asked him to get a therapist to certify that he'd be fine doing the training, which he did. A trainer also asked him to give them his word that he'd be okay. After completing the Basic and Advanced courses, Jeremy started Legacy, then quit. But as soon as he opted out, he said he began to receive phone calls from M.I.T.T. members, wondering why he was letting himself down. Jeremy called a friend outside M.I.T.T. She said he didn't sound safe. He decided he needed to get away, to leave California, and he headed for Boston, where another friend said he could crash. Even there, he couldn't sleep. He felt guilty for disappointing people. He started to wonder if people were stalking him. "I got really isolated and scared," he said. "I started feeling like I wouldn't be able to connect with anybody ever again."

A week after he arrived in Boston, Jeremy experienced a second psychotic break and threw himself into the Charles River. A police officer saw what happened and pulled him out. Jeremy spent a month in a hospital. Now he had a new job, a new apartment, a new city to call home. During a lull in conversation, talking about why he stuck it out, he said quietly, "A lot of the exercises put you in a victim mindset and then blame you for being there. Including any trauma that you've ever been through." He paused. "I honestly thought it would get better."

2.11 If there's one thing that connected many of the people I spoke to around my time with M.I.T.T., it's that they were searching. Searching for meaning. Searching for purpose. Just another human in their apartment at the end of the day. Members of my small group at M.I.T.T., led through rounds of tearful confessionals, said in so many words that to be a person in Los Angeles was to be an isolated person, an individual more exposed to risk than in other places: poverty, addictions, people who would take advantage. And not just exposed to risk—exposed generally. The Angeleno, like their freeway vehicle, had a hardened shell, one guy said, but it was thin and easy to ding. Without an accomplished career, a pretty partner to show off, what might a person claim?

To be a somebody without a something in Los Angeles meant you were a nobody—that's what these people made me think.

On day four of M.I.T.T., the room vented, spleened, and cried catharsis with glassy eyes. Aunt Lydia was the gaslight, peer pressure was the oxygen. I'd begun to doubt the premises of my skepticism, until finally I joined the wound culture. I told them, *I'm broken, I'm damaged, it's all my fault.* Even then, maybe I wasn't giving it everything. And even giving it my all, maybe I was still holding back, like I feared truly submitting to something that could radically improve my life.

Nope. It was stupid. Still, people drank it up. Maybe they were too exhausted to question the questioners. By two a.m. on my final night, having wept repeatedly again, having listened for days to people describe their darkest problems— sexual abuse, suicide attempts—I was done, driving home empty, albeit mildly stoned from an oxytocin super-high after the final exercise, where all 150 of us were encouraged to "heart hug" one another, embrace every single person in the room, one by one, over the course of an hour. And whether we imitated feelings of togetherness, mirroring them to one another, or actually experienced them, it didn't seem to matter, while Aunt Lydia told slushy anecdotes over the loudspeakers about people's lives being ruined, all to the tune of golden oldies playing in the background—song choices perhaps engraved in some Lifespring handbook from the late '70s, to make us weep.

Later, I brought up the choice of music with Marc Fisher, the *Washington Post* reporter. "They use those songs because they have the requisite emotional impact," he said. "They use the same techniques through the program because people come back for more and buy the next level. They don't even have to have a ridiculous origin story like the Scientologists. It's really pared down, simple, and effective."

In 1961, Martin Mayer wrote in *Esquire* that Los Angeles was "the home of the one-mind idea, beatnik or Buddhist or Bircher, and once the mind has found its idea it ceases to work." Several days into my M.I.T.T. training, Rachel started to worry about me. She was relieved on day five when I decided to sleep in. When M.I.T.T. telephoned, I didn't answer and went out to shop for groceries. Partly, I'll admit, because I'd acquired the idea that Jon, our small-group leader, might come looking for me. Two hours later, when he didn't show up, I actually felt disappointed. Aunt Lydia had told us repeatedly how, anytime we disengaged during the training, we'd failed not only ourselves but everyone else. I shot Jon an apologetic text, explaining my absence, and waited anxiously for his reply. He finally answered, "I'm sad that you won't be here today but I understand that everyone has their own journey and I appreciate how you played this week. You stayed open and I believe you got some great value and I hope it can lead you to continue diving deep."

I later talked to Nic, an aspiring actor, who attended the same Basic Training. Nic said he'd continued on into Advanced, then Legacy. "This literally saved me from so much pain in my life," he texted me. "Whether you believe it or not, this workshop changes lives for the better." I found a post of Nic's online, where he wrote that as a consequence of attending M.I.T.T., "I don't ever have to feel like someone that would be proud to live my life alone ever again."

I will admit, the day I quit M.I.T.T., after I received Jon's message, I almost drove back and rejoined.

False intimacy, real intimacy—all I knew was I craved something.

I was messed up about it for a week.

2.12 About a month later, Sonja, the woman who had introduced me to M.I.T.T in the first place, said, "I missed you at graduation." She'd gone to the final day of my training; it was going to be her big surprise, to celebrate that I'd made it through. "I was sad," she said. "I felt like you got off the roller-coaster before it got good."

I told her I found the training troubling on several fronts. First of all, the tax on people's minds and feelings, as well as the trainers' and staff's seeming lack of expertise in mental health. What I disliked most, I said, was the message I'd received, imparted through hours of conjured spontaneity, that M.I.T.T.'s "technology" was the best solution for traumatized people to repair their lives, yet its methods, cloaked in secrecy better suited to a magic trick, had been developed by a con man, repackaged by a hairdresser, and now were being guarded by an unpaid staff of fervent recruits. "It sounds like you don't believe other people had authentic experiences," she said. I said I thought of it like a horror movie, how a good director can set up a film so viewers are terrified at precise moments—which doesn't make the audience's fear in those moments less authentic, but it's still by design. I was sure that many people found the experience valuable in the glow of their sudden self-awareness, possibly for long after. That didn't mean it wasn't potentially dangerous, maybe very dangerous, for plenty more.

In Los Angeles, "reinvention is standard practice," the sociologist Manuel Pastor once said. In the months after my training, knowing that more trainings were taking place, I often wondered, could participants say no when they wanted to? The success of M.I.T.T. appeared to rely on a troubling premise: to get anything out of it, you needed to yield to all of it, despite rarely knowing what came next. The idea of consent became more like submission; the pressure inside the room to conform had been intense. *Submit and be revealed. Submit and be rewarded. Submit so that your problems finally can be cured.* Whereas saying no flew in the face of the training. "No" wasn't "giving it your all." "No" suggested that you didn't "acknowledge" some need deep inside you to be fixed in the first place.

Around that period, a friend's father introduced me to something called "ecstatic dance," wherein a large group of people gathered to dance for several hours. No drugs, no alcohol, no talking: the point was to get lost in the music and avoid interfering with other people's experiences. After I tried it for the first time, a friend said, "Do you realize your eyes are glowing?" The same day as M.I.T.T.'s graduation, a dance was scheduled near UCLA in an old Masonic lodge. The air was sedative, dimly golden. The music was very loud. I danced for two hours without stopping, until my clothes were drenched in sweat. At the end, the DJ finished with a dub song, a trip-hop song, then a brief moment of silence, which became "Simply Beautiful" by Al Green. I happen to love Al Green. Rachel had introduced me to his records; Al Green means a lot to us both. After all those hours of emotional meddling, I sat on the dance floor and cried for the umpteenth time. Though of all the recent tears, these were the sweetest. To be so shaken, to experience a response so authentically mine, the feeling was the opposite from so many moments that week.

To be moved is different from being manipulated.

2.13 Octavia E. Butler once described her imagination as "a radio imagination," suggesting one that listened, one that received messages from far-off lands.

In *Parable of the Sower*, perhaps the Butler novel most associated with Los Angeles, the city-state was on fire. Set in the 2020s, income inequality in L.A. had become murderous and the climate crisis was a destroyer of worlds. And in that setting lived a prophet, a young Black woman, Lauren Oya Olamina, whose calling was to lead a small band out to safety. Published in 1993, the book was prescient on a number of things: global warming, private communities, tragic fires. Then came *Sower*'s sequel, *Parable of the Talents*, in 1998, where the fictional country around Olamina had become riven by violence and paranoia and the president of the United States, an extreme conservative known to "scare, divide and bully people," enjoined his voters to "Help us to make America great again."

In her foreword to *Sower*'s recent rerelease, N. K. Jemisin wrote, "Butler does not appear to have intended the *Parable* novels to be a guidebook—and yet they are." Mike Davis, the historian, who had known Butler personally, thought she should be considered one of America's most important postwar writers, if only for enlarging our imagination about what was to come and how to address it. "Anyone can knock off a dystopia, especially if they're in L.A.," Davis told me. "But to explore what she did, and to have the hope at the end, in her writing, I think it's extraordinarily rare."

Even in Butler's later years, after so much success, her papers showed her still exhorting herself to connect with others. In a note from 2003, on her way to speak to students in Philadelphia, she wrote, "First and most important: Enjoy them. People are outrageous and ridiculous and fun. Invite them to enjoy you." Both through her fiction and in her diaries Butler demonstrated that no one was a nobody. To be a person in whatever place or time had value. Self-doubting, self-made, self-helped, the city-state's prophet suffered and thrived on things found in the world and mind. Both gave her pain. Both gave her art. *So be it. See to it.* She found a way.

LESSON 3

Some Are Footloose, Some Are Barnacles

A barrier at the border • North of the north,
east of the east • The human story in mango
soda • Where politics fail • "Are we breaking
the law?" • Scots, Catalans, Québécois,
Brexit campaigners • Mapping the internet
version of a nation • Tourists and surfaces
• Cartography through pointillism • Porous
borders • Interview with a king of Los Angeles
• Renaming a region • Vector Control • The
poet laureate of Lakewood • Narrow vs.
bigger • Latino Urbanism and the absence of
cozy • Possibility, space, hopefulness • Human
traffickers in Long Beach • Bridget "Biddy"
Mason • Storytelling as resistance

3.0 Early one morning, driving south, James Cordero described his grandfather's crossing story in terms of the Mexican Repatriation, the 1930s forced mass deportation from the United States of Mexicans and Mexican Americans. Robert A. Cordero had originally crossed in the '20s, part of one of the first waves pushed out, but he kept coming back. Cordero said his grandfather would sneak in, get caught, sneak in, get caught, same location, same agent, until the agent finally said, "If you do this one more time, you're going to be locked up for good." So his grandfather found another way in: he enlisted in the U.S. Army, kicked some ass, killed some Nazis. "And back then it was automatic," Cordero said. "You got your naturalization when you left the military."

On the highway, the early sunlight was so bright, cars around us looked like gold bricks. Cordero and his colleague Jacqueline Arellano, riding shotgun, told me they often spent their weekends doing their own sort of border crossing, not so much crossing as skirting. The two of them were trackers who scouted migrant trails in California's southern wilderness (I was asked not to reveal where) on behalf of a nonprofit organization called Border Angels that, among other activities, frequently led volunteers on aid missions into the mountains, to leave behind stores of water, food, and clothing to prevent people from dying from heatstroke in the summer, hypothermia in the winter, or dehydration year-round.

Enrique Morones, the Border Angels' founder, quoted the Bible that morning before we departed, Matthew 25:35. "For I was hungry and you gave me something to eat. I was thirsty and you gave me something to drink. I was a stranger and you invited me in."

In the car, Arellano explained that their work in the desert wasn't aiding and abetting, though sometimes it could seem close enough to put them at risk. In Tucson, a volunteer for a similar group, No More Deaths, faced felony charges for allegedly providing assistance to migrants trying to cross the Sonoran Desert. In July 2019, a jury refused to convict him. "I do not know what the government has hoped to accomplish here," the man told news cameras afterward. "I do know what the effect of all this has been and will continue to be: a raising of public consciousness, a greater awareness of the humanitarian crisis in the borderland, more volunteers who want to stand in solidarity with migrants, local residents stiffened in their resistance to border walls and the militarization of our communities, and a flood of water into the desert at a time when it is most needed."

The morning started to heat up. Cordero pulled over for gas. As far as he knew, he said, no one had died in their patch since Border Angels started its watch in the late 1990s. During the same period, estimates suggested thousands of people had died while trying to cross into the United States. Around the gas station, the landscape was moonlike, vastly empty. Signs of civilization were a few truckers, some litter blowing around. Cordero pointed into the distance. Out in the desert stood an isolated segment of

America's barrier-in-progress. It looked like a red brick wall, maybe a quarter mile long, a stockade in the middle of nowhere, disconnected. As if an enormous child had started to build something out of Lego and abruptly stopped.

That weekend, some miles away, a "caravan" of several thousand people from Central America had arrived in Tijuana, seeking admission into California. The president of the United States had labeled them "stone-cold criminals" and falsely suggested that their expedition was funded by a Jewish billionaire. At the direction of the White House, thousands of active-duty troops had been deployed, authorized to use lethal force. Meanwhile, planning documents obtained by *Newsweek* suggested that the U.S. military was more worried about the threat from the other side of the border. In a *Washington Post* interview, the president of the Texas Minutemen said, "We've proved ourselves before, and we'll prove ourselves again."

About half an hour later, after some light off-roading, Cordero parked next to a boulder in the foothills of an isolated mountain range. It felt as if we were standing on the edge of the country, on the edge of the edge. Two cars following us parked behind, carrying about a dozen volunteers. Everyone turned off their phones' tracking features. Suddenly a U.S. Border Patrol truck roared up the trail and stopped at twenty feet. Two agents stared at us, talking between themselves. "Where we're going today is public land," Cordero said loudly. He was imposing—tall, broad-shouldered, with a bushy beard. "It's my land. It's your land. Border patrol cannot check your identification without probable cause; that's a right you have as an American."

The agents reversed down the trail a moment later.

3.1 In the popular understanding—which is to say Anglo understanding, the frequently East Coast, masculine understanding that still underpinned public thought in the United States, a sense of American history more inclined toward pilgrims and cowboys than to green cards or diaries of the enslaved, the perspective of possessors and dominators who mostly had never been on the receiving end of conquest—the history of the city-state's place in national geography was often guided by a compass with destiny's magnet buried under the W.

"When I am in California," Theodore Roosevelt said in 1905, "I am not in the West. I am west of the West." Years later, the British painter and Los Angeles resident David Hockney would call Malibu "the edge of the Western world." A place that had once been Native American and Mexican was now mostly talked about in whiter terms—in part because the City of Angels had been, for a while, very white, both Anglo-inclined and Anglo-worshipful, appearing to many eyes as a unipolar place that had languidly transitioned from dreamy Spanish colonialism to mighty American democracy, all tied to the evocation of "going West" that was the rally cry for so-called pioneers, i.e., making it as much a matter of fantasy as orienteering, to be claimed by any "Okies" or pensioners from Iowa. And there was no lack of examples of L.A.'s whites being disinclined to acknowledge nonwhites, any non-Euro-seeming. In 1925, as recorded by William Alexander McClung in *Landscapes of Desire: Anglo Mythologies of Los Angeles*, the Allied Architects Association of Los Angeles endorsed a set of propositions stipulating "that the region is Mediterranean both ecologically and culturally; that its architecture and landscaping should perpetuate the 'collective memory' of Spain, Italy, and the south of France; that, however, the 'seductive influence' of those regions should merely influence, not dictate, architectural designs; that Southern California is a land of romance; but that its founding was 'sordid,' achieved not by Spanish aristocrats but by 'Indians, half breeds, and negroes, conscripts and undesirables.'" Such whitewashing even had its own term, *Spanish fantasy past*, suggesting a land found west of the Mediterranean, not north of the equator or east of the Pacific. As Joan Didion wrote in "Notes from a Native Daughter," "It is characteristic of Californians to speak grandly of the past as if it had simultaneously begun, *tabula rasa*, and reached a happy ending on the day the wagons started west."

And yet the city-state would not be so colonized. Modern Los Angeles was a metropolis of émigrés, refugees, and striving hearts—*the* city of immigrants, a radically multipolar place of individuals from other lands. "Their arrival changed it from a small and little known city of fifty thousand people into the largest and most renowned of Pacific coast centers" (Robert Fogelson, *Fragmented Metropolis*). "Era un gran pueblo magnético . . . era un gran tiempo de hibridos" (Rockdrigo Gonázalez, "Tiempo de Hibridos"). Really, the saga of the city-state was better imagined from other directions, principally as a northerly place, for people arriving from places south, where Los Angeles was the hemisphere's northernmost Spanish-speaking megalopolis, a sprawling basin of plazas and churches, with a climate familiar to people from El Salvador, Guatemala, or Honduras, for whom California was always el norte. "Los Angeles is for the American Southwest and Mexico's northern third what Mexico City is to the southern and central regions of Mexico proper," Lester Langley wrote in *Mexamerica: Two Countries, One Future.* During a roundtable discussion, the journalist Carolina Miranda once said, "It was never the last stop. It was the first. It was the beginning." In Luis J. Rodríguez's memoir *Always Running: La Vida Loca: Gang Days in L.A.,* his father tells his mother, "I'll never go back to Mexico. I'd rather starve here. You want to stay with me, it has to be in Los Angeles. Otherwise, go."

None of this should omit the L.A. that was a locus for people headed east, voyagers from the Philippines, Thailand, Japan, Korea, Bangladesh, China, and more; people who also weren't privileged in official storytelling as the Spaniards and white Americans were. And that's not to forget any Russians, Iranians, Samoans, Ethiopians, or Armenians; not to forget, though we had forgotten, the people who were here previously, the Tongva, the Chumash, approximately sixty thousand Native people who lived in coastal California when Spanish colonization began in the 1770s—a population that, according to John Mack Faragher's *Eternity Street: Violence and Justice in Frontier Los Angeles,* fell by nearly two-thirds within fifty years.

People for whose ancestors the mission bells that now decorated California's highways—artifacts from an imaginary Spanish heritage—might plausibly toll, *We invaded, we enslaved, we destroyed.*

The point being, to get a feeling of where the borders of the city-state were located, where they existed in space and time—historically, presently, outside of time as well, despite all the efforts at cultural cryogenics—it felt important to start a hundred and fifty miles south of Downtown, in the wilderness.

3.2 Anthropogeography, also known as human geography, is the branch of geography that deals with people and communities, how cultures move and change. And in the desert wilderness, as we hiked, Arellano and Cordero both suggested that if the imagination stretched even slightly beyond two-dimensional topography, the dirt under our boots could easily be called L.A. dirt, the border an L.A. border. Which seemed fitting considering even the mayor of the city-state had previously called L.A. "the northernmost city of Latin America" and meant it as a compliment; Los Angeles remained a gate for families traveling from San Salvador or Guatemala City in search of better pay, better odds, or mere safety.

What right had anyone to citizenship by chance of birth?

Wasn't the southern border just another expression of America's love for race restrictions?

Under heavy sunlight, I was thinking the future of borders, at least conceptually, probably had more to do with lines of no thickness—firewalls around our data, not walls in the sand—but why was a feeling of "home" something I had lucked into, that others were forced to earn? Deserts had few partitions anyway, so no wonder I was reminded of the city-state; as an urban settlement, a lack of constraining walls had been a major player in Los Angeles's growth as it oozed over the landscape in the manner of a Berlin, a London, a Tokyo.

"The rampant proliferation of the immense megalopolis

that is Tokyo gives the impression of a silkworm eating a mulberry leaf" (Yoshinobu Ashinara, *L'ordre caché: Tokyo, la ville du XXIe siècle*).

In the afternoon, Arellano discovered an empty tampon box under a bush. All day, we'd found discarded sweatshirts, lipstick tubes, crumpled cans of Herdez mango soda. At one point, someone picked up a child's *Star Wars* trading card, and one woman stepped away to cry. Several people in the group, mostly twentysomethings, had crossing stories of their own, Arellano told me. "For our generation, there's a disconnect with how did we get here. I'm seeing from the younger generation, they're really owning their history. Their indigenous roots, their migrant roots. People are asking their families, 'Who the hell am I?'" One woman told me she was on the trail because she'd come to the U.S. as a kid and now worked as a mental health counselor for immigrants. "I have this one woman in mind," she said. "I was working with her child, and the story of her immigration came up. She told me when she crossed, she was twelve. The group got separated. She was lucky she had someone [to guide her], she said; she was begging him that she didn't want to continue, and he didn't allow it. He said, 'We all go, or nobody does.'" The woman took a deep breath. "It's like, hearing that—yes, I can do more. I do it for her."

Throughout the day the group left behind jugs of water and packages of food, then filled trash bags with old caches, some used and discarded, some not discovered. Cordero said they'd had their water bottles cut open many times, possibly by people who disagreed with their mission, possibly by Border Patrol. From *The Line Becomes a River: Dispatches from the Border*, the 2018 memoir by Francisco Cantú, a former Border Patrol agent: "It's true that we slash their bottles and drain their water into the dry earth, that we dump their backpacks and pile their food and clothes to be crushed and pissed on and stepped over, strewn across the desert and set ablaze."

"A policeman's job is only easy in a police state" (*Touch of Evil*).

3.3   In the desert, immigration didn't feel like a topic, something to be argued about. The border felt like an equator, a battle site, a place where politics had failed.

Borders were war.

3.4   In the afternoon we spotted footprints. Cordero guessed they were two days old and suggested that I imagine they were mine, that I'd been hiking for weeks, when maybe I'd never walked more than ten miles in my life. Feelings of anxiety and fear, fear of agents, thugs, pandilleros, corrupt cops—so hungry, so thirsty, so dirty and dusty, maybe sick from fever, bowel problems, heat exhaustion. Worrying about Border Patrol, agents equipped with thermal imaging equipment like you saw in the movies, helicopters in the sky that could spot footprints, sensors in the dirt that could hear footsteps. Maybe I'd wound up barefoot because my sneakers broke down, maybe my sneakers melted. At any point I could be robbed, raped, bitten by a snake, all while I'm climbing boulders in the dark, scrambling away from sudden whips of light. I might break a leg, and all for what?

I found myself wondering, had I ever wanted something so badly?

At the end of the day, the sunlight was still searing but

more leaden. The group packed out trash bags while helicopters buzzed overhead. Arellano and Cordero drove half an hour to a tavern on the side of the road to grab dinner. "For those of us whose background includes privilege, being documented in the United States, something that people are literally dying to get—we have an obligation," Arellano said. "The way we'd wish if the shoe were on the other foot. They're human beings. I did absolutely nothing but be born in L.A. to deserve the right to be here."

"*Deserve*," Cordero intoned, laughing, putting his arm around her.

"It was a complete luck of the draw," Arellano said, shaking her head in wonder.

3.5 Sometimes human geography is derived from blood and treaties. Sometimes it is influenced by epidemics. Sometimes it is carved out by social diseases like pass laws or redlining. Sometimes it is a matter of nationalism combined with devolution—Catalans, Québécois, even Brexit campaigners—when provinces want more of their own say, or only their own say.

Around Los Angeles, sometimes human geography is difficult to comprehend, but you still feel it, like the edges of a ghost.

3.6 For the physicist and satellite engineer Dan Gutierrez, the geography of Los Angeles County, human or otherwise, suggested a city-state, yes, but more so its "internet version," he thought, by which he meant networks upon networks layered densely in a mesh to form larger networks of neighborhoods, lateral villages, little towns overlapping, streets woven through them like fiber strands, such that driving from one place to another around Greater Los Angeles felt like social media's infinite scroll. Then, on top of that, even more layers! Shimmering cobwebs of social connections, city services, layers as thin as nets used by trapeze artists and comparably woven with holes, holes of regular yet different shapes, such that different-size people might fall through one net but be saved by the next, though some people just kept falling, Gutierrez thought, falling, falling, falling, unprotected, unsaved, through hole after hole after hole—and *that's* what living in Los Angeles felt like.

It was just after sunrise, an autumn Saturday, and Gutierrez said all this while climbing a staircase, perhaps his twelfth or fifteenth staircase that morning. "I think about this quite a bit when I'm doing these walks," he said a moment later over his shoulder. "But I don't always have someone to talk about it with."

For all of that, he was not out of breath.

"Here in Los Angeles the shape of the city is soft at the edges, piled layer on layer, cloud on cloud," Charles Moore wrote in *The City Observed, Los Angeles* (1984). Gutierrez, from San Pedro, was a scientist professionally, but was perhaps better known as a climber of stairs. Several years prior, he'd envisioned a border for the city-state composed of public staircases strung together, a phantom perimeter going up and down, up and down around the fragmented metropolis—a circular borderline of about 310 miles, climbing thirty-three thousand feet over 760 sets of steps. By the time we met, Gutierrez had hiked his imaginary border once in entirety, and he was in the midst of repeating it in weekend segments. That morning, he and a couple of friends were climbing what

Gutierrez dubbed "Segment I," a twenty-mile trail involving ninety public stairways through Edendale, Angelino Heights, and Westlake North, with approximately 5,000 up steps and 3,640 feet of elevation gain, that ended at the original Tommy's, one of Gutierrez's favorite local burger stands.

Hong Kong, Shenzhen, New York—monuments to the vertical. L.A. had its skyscrapers and mountains, but predominantly it was flat, rooted laterally, stripmalled from the Pacific Ocean to Palm Springs. "It's like Los Angeles, the car parks tend to find you, wherever you are" (J. G. Ballard, *Super-Cannes*). Still, it had plenty of stairs.

Gutierrez wore hiking shorts, sneakers, and a wide-brimmed hat. His stairs were any set that a citizen wouldn't get into trouble for climbing: three steps leading from a sidewalk to a bank; eighteen steps to reach the top of a set of bleachers. Some of the taller staircases around Los Angeles, a hundred-plus steps, had been constructed so that residents of hilly neighborhoods could reach their morning commute back when streetcars were employed. What Gutierrez loved, he said, was the sense of circumnavigating a place so hard to fathom. It wasn't about the sights along the way, but the way itself. "To see the city from this perspective gives you an entirely different understanding."

Asked if he ever got tired of looking at stairs (after only a couple of hours, I was definitely tired of looking at stairs), he said, "I look at them as atoms within a compound. I'm not into the aesthetics as much as some." This recalled *Rider's California: A Guide Book for Travelers, With 28 Maps and Plans* (1925)—a first edition I found in the Los Angeles Public Library that crumbled at the touch—when a Southern California Chamber of Commerce officer told the author, "I see that you lay emphasis on the esthetic side. That doesn't interest us much around here."

For hours, the group would hike one set of stairs, then walk to the next, climb those stairs, or descend them—stairs that, without Gutierrez's needlepoint, might have met the fate of, well, stairs: a way to divvy up vertical space; a measurement of something else, rather than things in themselves. Gutierrez's stairs were loved.

3.7 The layout of the city-state is difficult to explain to outsiders—how it's laid out, how to explore it—because it is difficult for virtually anybody to understand. Here inland, here shore, here gated enclave, here slum.

The theorist Walter Benjamin once wrote, "To articulate the past historically does not mean to recognize it 'the way it really was' (Ranke). It means to seize hold of a memory as it flashes up at a moment of danger." But for those without memory, without connection, they're left to surfaces. In Los Angeles, the tourist would be pointed to the Walk of Fame, not Watts; the Venice Boardwalk, not the barrio. And tourists made relatable mistakes. They assumed neighborhoods were the same for being contiguous. They assumed that only one car should make a left as a light turned red. They didn't know to drive up to Chatsworth or go buy books in Leimert Park. They didn't know the tones of shadows on Union Station's walls.

At the same time, locals weren't exactly protected from falling into clichés. The author Stefan Kiesbye, author of *Berlingeles*, once said in an interview, "When [my wife and I] moved from Koreatown to Long Beach, we lost all our friends, as though there really was a wall around the neighborhoods."

3.8 "L.A. is not a city that presents itself to you," Sam Sweet, a local amateur historian, told me one gray afternoon. "It rewards you to the degree that you're willing to unlock it. That's always been the beauty of the city for me."

Sweet specialized in a pointillist style: a history of Los Angeles told through a series of booklets he self-published, called *All Night Menu*, each of them eight stories long, each story having an address for a title, revealing the biography of what made that place unique: 501 N. Mednik, in Maravilla, home to the city-state's oldest handball court; 207 Ashland Avenue, in Ocean Park, where the artist Richard Diebenkorn once painted; 1950 North Central Avenue, a roller rink called Skateland that was practically the birthplace of N.W.A. Sweet and I met in late November, at a diner in Cypress Park—La Abeja at 3700 North Figueroa Street—and ordered coffee and quesadillas. In the background, Frank Sinatra sang "Have Yourself a Merry Little Christmas." Sweet was a thoughtful white guy with reddish hair under a black Dodgers hat. He was fairly skeptical about my project. Not that a city-state was wrongheaded, Sweet thought, he just preferred to work in miniature, to take it one address at a time. He sat in silence for a long moment. "One of the most profound gifts of Los Angeles is that it forces you to reckon with the truth of impermanence," he said. "What more essential challenge is there than to recognize and hopefully absorb the truth of impermanence? This is something that short-circuits people. Emotionally, I agree with preservationists, but philosophically, nothing can be preserved. Even the geology in California, the earth upon which the city is built, is defined by its constant state of fluctuation."

I asked Sweet to characterize how he envisioned his place in the great expanse. He stared around the restaurant. "A relationship with a city is like being in a relationship with a person," he said. "I never find Los Angeles lacking in anything. When people accuse it of being deficient, that's self-reflection. In L.A., there's always a way. L.A. is an organism that provides, but it demands initiation. When you get passive, it's easy to disappoint yourself."

A few weeks earlier, during my day of stair-climbing, Gutierrez would often call out, like a slightly winded clairvoyant, the number of stairs of other staircases nearby. *That set behind the parking lot: 201 stairs. That one down the block: 198.* He also generally didn't experience the disorientation even Angelenos sometimes felt, as if his memory contained both a map of the county and an almanac of its cement. Late that day, while the former Queen of Angels Hospital loomed above us, Gutierrez was asked how many staircases he kept in his mind at any given moment. "Hundreds? More? I can be anywhere in the county and point out a set of stairs somewhere nearby." He added a moment later, nervously laughing, "I'm ruined, I know."

There was a funny thing about Los Angeles I'd begun to notice while touring the county: you might not know where you were exactly, yet it almost always looked, smelled, even felt like L.A., as though Los Angeles were a floating experience. The French novelist Honoré de Balzac described something similar in his 1833 novel *Ferragus*, finding a "space without a name, the neutral space of Paris. There, Paris is no longer; and there, Paris still lingers. The spot is a mingling of street, square, boulevard, fortification, garden, avenue, high-road, province, and metropolis; certainly, all of that is to be found there, and yet the place is nothing of all that,—it is a desert."

3.9 A border's contours are intended to exclude and include, but in the city-state they seem especially porous. And when the president of the United States, soon after moving into the White House, issued an executive order to intensify a clampdown on immigration, the mayor of Los Angeles, along with other mayors of large American cities, defied him.

But for all the mayor's powers, not inconsiderable, the man who was mayor of Los Angeles—since 1850, it had always been a man, from Alpheus P. Hodges to Eric Garcetti, including the tenure of senior Ku Klux Klan member John Porter and also three terms for Meredith P. Snyder, nicknamed "Pinky," referring to the shade of his sideburns—often wound up being less chief executive and more cheerleading captain, subject to the whims of the (occasionally corrupt) Los Angeles City Council.

The point being, by no means was the mayor of Los Angeles some kind of king.

3.10 And lo, in the beginning, there was nothing before the men but a magnificent destiny to be harvested from the ground and from the sea. Inevitably, also some Mexicans lingering around, some old bear flags needing burning, a population of Native people to be slaughtered—but look, gold!

And over many years of pans panning, nooses lynching, fortunes made, the State of California was established, and swiftly the men saw it organized, subdivided into counties to be overseen, in most cases, by men like themselves, men who would nobly manage the cumbersome tasks of statehood, things like law enforcement, public health, public safety, and education in their regions—like Los Angeles, for example, "Queen of the Cow Counties," which then was basically a farm town with fewer than two thousand people, most of them involved in agriculture, overseeing some of the largest herds of cattle in the state. According to the historian Leonard Pitt, an Austrian visitor wrote in 1878, "No happier paradise for the farmer can be found than Los Angeles County."

Today's Austrian visitor would find Greater Los Angeles a paradise (or not) for a much bigger population—more than ten million human beings, few of them involved with agriculture, and a mere 6,889 cattle, according to the 2017 Census of Agriculture—and yet the government remained the same: a kingdom of five blocs, each with its own ruler, "five little kings" who individually ruled over some two million humans each for up to three four-year terms, and they almost always served out those terms. (The three-term limit wasn't imposed until 2002. Previously there were no limits, and supervisors basically ruled for life.) "It's the most bizarre form of government known to man," Zev Yaroslavsky, a little king from 1994 to 2014, told me. "Unless you're one of the five."

In population, the city-state was bigger than most U.S. states. For example, New Jersey. What if New Jersey were to replace its government, throw away the governor, the senate, general assembly, and all the legislators, and replace them with a five-member board. Would anyone think it was a good idea?

During his career, Yaroslavsky wielded power around town for four decades, nearly twenty years on the Los Angeles City Council, then a two-decade term as supervisor. Life as a little king, he said, had been something of a turf war: five individuals reluctant to interfere with one another's districts—a game of not touching the others' thrones, basically—with everyone looking for consensus. "It feels like finding the lowest common denominator, which is always the least precise number," Yaroslavsky said.

When defenders stood up for the five-king system—to be accurate for recent days, a system of five queens—speed was cited, a lack of checks and balances allowing problems to be tackled more swiftly. But problems to match were endemic: a system of political patronage with little accountability, a parachute drag on decision-making. The game of kingdoms meant that difficult issues could go unaddressed for years or even decades. A failing hospital, a homelessness crisis countywide, all while blue-ribbon commissions filed their reports.

Since his retirement, Yaroslavsky had called for a single person to run the county, a chief executive accountable to voters, but he didn't see it happening anytime soon; a spectrum of power players, already rewarded, not to mention the five supervisors, would need to find it compelling. "Government can be highly inefficient under the best of circumstances," he said at one point. "Government by committee is far from optimal." When we spoke, Yaroslavsky was still mourning the death of his wife. Barbara Yaroslavsky died in 2018 while recovering from—of all things—a West Nile virus infection acquired from a mosquito bite at their L.A. home. These days, Yaroslavsky's work included helping oversee UCLA's annual Quality of

Life Index. He said that a recent survey, in 2019, had asked people, in so many words, if Los Angeles was the kind of place where the rich got richer and the average person had no chance, or if L.A. was someplace where, if you worked hard, you could be whatever you want. "Fifty-five percent of all respondents said the rich get richer. People thirty-nine and under, it's sixty-four percent," Yaroslavsky told me. "Young people have far too little hope in this county."

It's said that nations bind people together by the memory of what they'd once been, not exactly what they are presently. The idea had an echo in the city-state, I thought, if a tinny one. Governments grow from their environment, but few regions had grown like Los Angeles while its government hardly grew at all. The society that constitutes the city-state today—so atomized, so homogenized—seemed connected less by shared memory than by a collective sense of us all having somehow wound up living in the same boarding-house, atop rotting stilts.

3.11 "Because we have known nothing else, the words *democracy, politics, liberty* define our mental horizon, but we are no longer sure that we know them in a real sense, and our attachment to them has more to do with reflex than with reflection" (Jean-Marie Guéhenno, *The End of the Nation-State*).

Geography is often a word game. To history's so-called victors go the marketing rights, not to mention the power. El Pueblo de Nuestra Señora la Reina de los Ángeles, the Town of Our Lady the Queen of the Angels, was the Spanish pueblo founded in 1781. Under Mexican rule, it became the regional capital of Alta California, for the first time a ciudad, no longer el pueblo. After the Mexican-American War, as the United States pursued its imperialist drive, Los Angeles became the boomtown that kept on booming—cattle to citrus, oil to real estate, Hollywood to health cures—for which writers developed all sorts of takes. Christopher Isherwood said it was "antiseptic, heartless, hateful, neon-mirage." For Lynell George, "broken edges and patched-together lives." Rarely simply itself, Los Angeles often would be summoned to express another: a midwestern suburb; a Pacific Rim metropole; a heteropolis—suggesting a land full of love for difference and all things weird: sideways skyscrapers, pluralization, chicken shawarma burritos. For some it was simpler. "It's Houston plus porn," one journalist told me in a Spring Street bar.

Some of the earliest naming, at least by Europeans, came in 1542, when two ships sailing under Spanish colors gave history Baya de los Fumos, bay of smoke, inspired, some believed, by fires burning in the coastal villages of the Tongva people—those same people who would be drawn into debt, enslaved, decimated by infectious disease, and also hunted for sport. In the 1850s alone, according to *Murder State: California's Native American Genocide, 1846–1873*, by Brendan C. Lindsay, the state of California paid millions of dollars in what was essentially bounty money, later reimbursed by the federal government, to anyone who killed Native people—a pastime so common, the *San Diego Herald* noted on October 7, 1853, a visitor might think shooters were practicing for duels.

Over time, the Native people responded ferociously, burning missions, winning battles, all in a region that had been turned into a death trap against them. "The hapless Franciscans presided over a genuine holocaust, a tragic genocide that marks the first great crime against humanity known to the history of this region" (Philip J. Ethington, *A Companion to Los Angeles*).

3.12 Any kingdom requires hinterlands as part of its definition. In this author's estimation, it takes more than a hundred miles in any direction from Downtown for a sense of the city-state to dissipate—around Lompoc, Bakersfield, or San Diego, maybe—and yet some aspects are still felt on the wind.

The Greater Los Angeles County Vector Control District served more than a million homes, businesses, and weed-infested lots under its assignment to defend the citizenry from contagions. In its mission, it deployed pickup trucks to explore underground storm drains; jeeps fitted with plow blades to attack concrete channels where those drains dumped trash; a squadron of "sentinel chickens," flocks of fowl scattered around the county that waited to be infected and warn us of invasion. The inspectors were like a special ops team that few know about, fighting daily to save Los Angeles from a deadly outbreak that could kill us all. "We're kind of the tip of the spear," said Mark Daniel, Vector Control's director of operations.

According to Timothy C. Winegard, author of *The Mosquito: A Human History of Our Deadliest Predator*, mosquitoes had killed more people than any other single cause of death in human history. Being "vectors," as they're known in the industry, mosquitoes could carry and transmit viral diseases such as yellow fever and chikungunya. They were responsible for outbreaks of dengue in Bangladesh and Zika in Brazil—and were increasingly showing up around Los Angeles, where mosquitoes typically hadn't been a problem.

"People are saying, 'Wait a second, do I live in Florida now?'"
Daniel said. He explained that what made L.A. County particularly scary for his team was its anthropogeography, the
human geography that called bullshit on Southern California's topographical demarcations: so many fluctuating popu-
lations, so many people on the go.

Also because, season after season, their call logs kept
growing.

At Vector Control's headquarters, mosquito sculptures
were displayed in cabinets like so many hunting trophies.
Daniel explained that the *Aedes albopictus*, aka the Asian
tiger mosquito, was believed to have arrived in Los Angeles
around 2001 after a surge of interest in "lucky bamboo," a
popular indoor plant shipped in from overseas. As exports
were packed into shipping containers, aedes tagged along.

For Vector Control, to protect meant to patrol. A pair of
Daniel's inspectors, Mary Campbell and Yessenia Curiel,
rolled out to visit homes. The first was in Southeast L.A.
Wearing a shiny badge, Campbell rang the doorbell. She
liked her job because it felt like a mission, she said, helping
people avert catastrophe; mosquitoes bit everyone, rich or
poor, and were biting more people than ever. To illustrate
the point, she pointed to a tray of jars against the house.
Aedes mosquitoes could breed in something as small as a
bottle cap, and the eggs might lie dormant for years, only to
be reanimated when adequately warm and wet. Here each
jar was full of water; inside were mosquito larvae.

When nobody answered the bell, they left a notice saying they'd be back. People not answering the door happened
a lot, Campbell explained, especially in neighborhoods
where residents might fear a visit from immigration. In fact,
Vector Control had recently changed their uniforms to look

less like law enforcement, all because they needed to speak to people. The next house, five minutes away, was worse. On a street of modest suburban homes, it looked like a gutter punk garden center. The front yard was a jungle of fish tanks, plants in tires. Curiel picked up a watering can lined with mosquito eggs. The owner arrived, an older Asian gentleman, and Campbell gently informed him that his neighbors had complained about mosquitoes. "I see them once in a while," he said defensively, then reluctantly let them see his backyard. It was a hoarder's rain forest. Discarded furniture, brimming boxes. Campbell grabbed a bucket off the ground and switched on her flashlight. Inside were hundreds of mosquito eggs. "It's a nightmare scenario," she whispered.

Their boss, Mark Daniel, arrived at the house and tipped down his sunglasses. Tall with a goatee and a gravelly voice, Daniel closely resembled Jeff Bridges playing The Dude in *The Big Lebowski*, though with a melancholic air. In the coming weeks, his investigators would return to check on progress. If the owner didn't comply, there could be fines of up to $1,000 a day. Countywide, the battle seemed uphill, if not impossible, I said—a challenge requiring eradication, constant education—but Campbell and Curiel had been cheerful and upbeat, not at all discouraged, even if an outbreak was only a matter of time. "What sets my team apart is their willingness to show up," Daniel said. "These people really want to help people. That makes it worth it." He added a moment later, "It can be enough at the end of the day."

3.13 Not far away, in the county's southeast corner, was Lakewood, a town practically built overnight. Construction began in 1950 on empty fields. Three years later, there were more than seventy thousand residents. New houses had been finished every seven and a half minutes.

The city-state's "instant city," Lakewood in the present day was still quintessentially suburban: a grid of streets with uniform lots, similar-looking houses, boulevards with landscaped medians running unfailingly straight. Lakewood possessed the oldest fully enclosed shopping mall in the United States. It was where the first Denny's was built. It was also where, in 1993, nine boys from the local high school were accused of being members of a "Spur Posse," assigning points for sex, and were arrested on rape charges, charges that were eventually dropped against eight of the nine.

And Lakewood was also where D. J. Waldie, the city's former deputy city manager and the author of a poetic memoir called *Holy Land*, among other works, had lived for almost all of his life in the same 957-square-foot house that his parents purchased in 1946. Which meant that the streets Waldie walked each day for a little more than seventy years were frequently the same streets, many views the same views, trees the same trees under similar light at different times of year.

On Lakewood's first day of home sales, Waldie told me, an estimated thirty thousand people had lined up to inspect model houses. "And the lots," he said in a rhythmic timbre, "fifty feet wide by a hundred feet deep, almost uniformly across the city, grid out right-angle street blocks, over and over and over again." The homes were cookie-cutter by nature, though buyers could choose from fifty-two different exteriors, for which there were thirty-nine color combinations. "As a consequence of slight differences in this regular pattern you get an interesting, low-key tension between sameness and variation," he said.

Other communities in the city-state—Panorama City, Irvine—had been comparably spawned or dropped into place, but not quite with Lakewood's scale or speed. Did people in Lakewood think of themselves as living in Los Angeles? "They absolutely do not think of themselves as living in Los Angeles," Waldie said. "People who live here make a distinction between the municipal boundaries of the City of Los Angeles and the bigger thing called L.A., which extends into Orange County, out almost into the desert. We know we live in L.A., but we also know we don't live in Los Angeles."

"The acquisitive city-state grabbed at everything in its horizons and drew it under its rule: lands, townships, castles, people," wrote the historian Lauro Martines in *Power and Imagination: City-states in Renaissance Italy.* Waldie explained that Greater Los Angeles had acquired its shape in a similar manner, especially around Lakewood and nearby Long Beach: grabbing, hoarding, seizing power. What about a sense of rootedness, I wondered, how some people around L.A. seemed uprooted while others were so fixedly settled. Waldie nodded in agreement. One of the most visible things that had changed over his years in Lakewood, he said, was its population. Now home to Filipino families, Latina families, Chinese American families, in the beginning the town had been white by design, mostly thanks to racist lending practices, but also discriminatory sales practices. "Southern California was very southern," Waldie said. "You have a lot of small-town and semirural midwesterners and southerners arriving between 1920 and 1960, and their attitudes about race were not far from those found in the Old South. And that was once characteristic of Lakewood too, so many southerners and border southerners moved here in the 1950s."

Of course, those practices were hardly exclusive to Lakewood, or without broad contemporary impact. Between 2013 and 2017, according to the Brookings Institution's "segregation index," Los Angeles was the tenth most segregated metro area in the United States. (Milwaukee, New York, and Chicago were the top three.) Santa Monica, particularly its northern end, remained deeply segregated, i.e., almost completely white. In *Black Los Angeles: American Dreams and Racial Realities*, the sociologist Darnell Hunt found two restrictions on the original deed for his first home in Baldwin Hills, built in 1953, that weren't uncommon in Los Angeles at that time: "1. No part of any said realty shall ever be sold, conveyed, leased, or rented to any person not of the white or Caucasian race. 2. No part of any said realty shall ever at any time be used or occupied or be permitted to be used or occupied by any person not of the white or Caucasian race, except such as are in the employ of the resident owner or resident tenants of said property."

The slogan of Lakewood was "Times change. Values don't." And yet it was far more varied than when it started, Waldie said, both in population and appearance. A more Latino aesthetic generally, and one that exhibited the same signs as the rest of L.A.: Dodger flags, Lakers decals, WE BUY HOUSES, DUPLEX FOR SALE, COMPRO CASAS CASH. Perhaps Lakewood's design actually encouraged diversity, or at least neighborliness? Waldie weighed the idea. "Because it's Southern California, we're outdoors a good deal," he said. "For a lot of the year, and throughout the history of the city, Lakewood people are out and about, and they see each other. That may tone down the 'otherness.' If you see your neighbor every weekend puttering around in their garden, they don't seem that 'other,' maybe. But I don't claim more than I should."

"In the suburbs, a manageable life depends on a compact among neighbors. The unspoken agreement is an honest hypocrisy," Waldie wrote in *Holy Land*. That "hypocrisy" referred to something small and specific—ordinances in a town's municipal code that went unenforced—but felt bigger, when I drove Lakewood's grids, more like the silent agreement required by tolerance: the recognition that, to be neighbors in a city-state, people need to tolerate the difficult, the thorny, the abnormal. As someone who found change more comfortable than permanence, I remarked that I saw Waldie's endurance in a single town as being noteworthy, his truly being *of a place*. He looked out the window. For a brief moment he seemed flustered. "It's not too much to say that some people, and I'm one of them, are made for connection to a place that endures," Waldie said. "Some people are footloose, and some people are barnacles. I'm a barnacle."

All of his life, a feeling of home had been a habit, Waldie told me at one point, something deep inside that came out each day. When we met, he wore a sharp gray jacket and crisp white shirt, his hair neatly combed—a person precise in his appearance and speech. Waldie said quietly at the end of my visit, "In terms of my relationship with the city, with place, I am and have always been at peace with what I am here. With what it is as I understand it." He paused and laughed to himself. "It might be laid as a charge against me that I'm either lazy or provincial, but I'm not made in opposition. I'm made in connection."

3.14 "The critics of the suburbs say that you and I live narrow lives. I agree. My life is narrow. From one perspective or another, all our lives are narrow. Only when lives are placed side by side do they seem larger" (D. J. Waldie, *Holy Land*).

3.15 Days after my Lakewood visit, the urban planner and activist James Rojas met me for coffee and pie at Philippe's Downtown. Rojas, born and raised in East Los Angeles, studied city planning at the Massachusetts Institute of Technology after serving abroad in the army. "I had no idea that city planning existed as a profession and what it entailed," he said. "I just thought, 'I love Paris, therefore city planning should be fun.'" At the time, he explained, urban planning often divided cities into good and bad, such as Paris: good, Detroit: bad. As a planner, particularly as a Latino planner, Rojas wanted to enlarge his practice beyond his formal education to incorporate what he'd experienced growing up in 1960s and '70s Boyle Heights and East Los Angeles.

In his 1938 essay "Urbanism as a Way of Life," Louis Wirth wrote, "Because the city is the product of growth rather than of instantaneous creation, it is to be expected that the influences which it exerts upon the modes of life should not be able to wipe out completely the previously dominant modes of human association." Rojas's practice was rooted in what he labeled Latino Urbanism—social cohesion, street-facing aesthetics, how ways of life brought north had been translated in Los Angeles County. It could mean a Catholic shrine on a sidewalk in South Gate. An outdoor altar showcasing military medals in City Terrace. A teenager's homemade posters for punk shows in East Long Beach. It came back to the idea of a plaza, Rojas said, with all of its social activity. "I examined the artifacts Latinos left behind that helped support social cohesion in their communities," he said. "A sofa on a porch, tables and chairs in the front yard, the front-yard fence—they help Latinos use outdoor space and promote social interaction similar to café seating on a Paris sidewalk!"

"Los Angeles is profoundly more experimental than other cities," Dana Cuff, the founding director of cityLAB at UCLA, told me. "That comes from being a city that isn't codified by nineteenth-century formats. We look west, rather than east, for references. We look south. We're not Eurocentric. Asia, the Americas, those are our axes and networks."

In Rojas's view, one thing that distinguished Los Angeles aesthetically from other big American cities was its lack of coziness. As a metroplex—both cosmopolitan and parochial, city and country—the city-state often required admirers to find beauty in places where lines between public and private blurred, and in those spaces little was found of the fine-grain texture of San Francisco or Manhattan, the visual warmth of a Minneapolis, a Boston. Instead, L.A. was broadly harsh, all concrete and fences, sand and grit, studded by emblems of fortification. However, if an observer got down to the neighborhood level, especially in Latino neighborhoods, they might discover the social capital of people spending time with one another. A family cookout in a driveway. The sound of taqueros in Whittier. It was a version of well-being, Rojas thought, that grew organically, not by imposed design. "Urban planning land-use policies and urban design guidelines need to be inclusive and embrace different ways of being in the city rather than taking a one-size-fits-all approach," he said.

"Like other women in our street, each morning Mrs. Santos raked the front yard, sprinkled water on it to keep dust down, then trimmed her geraniums," Mary Helen Ponce wrote in *Hoyt Street*, her memoir about growing up in Pacoima. "Still other casitas sported a porch swing where, on warm summer evenings, adults gossiped or told stories of la Llorona to pesky children, the soft Spanish words drifting down Hoyt Street and dissolving into the night."

3.16 At a large party in Texas during a book festival, I didn't know anybody, so I introduced myself to the closest stranger. Michael Frank was visiting from New York City to promote *The Mighty Franks*, a memoir he wrote about growing up in Los Angeles, he explained, though much of the book was about visiting his grandmothers, who had lived together in a two-story apartment building below Laurel Canyon, on North Ogden Drive, just above Sunset Boulevard, number 1648.

Which made for a shock when I told Frank that the apartment Rachel and I were renting at that point was also below Laurel Canyon, on North Ogden Drive, just above Sunset, number 1648—and our apartment, we quickly figured out, was *the* apartment, same floor, same layout: an apartment where, before we signed the lease, the landlord had told us he didn't care about a credit check, but he needed to know our favorite colors and astrological signs, to see if we'd be a good fit for the building's vibes.

Anyway, it was a strange coincidence.

"Is it important that I come from L.A.?" Frank asked me months later after we struck up a correspondence. "In the East, where I live now, it seems more important to people I meet than to me. 'You're not a typical Angeleno'—I used to hear this quite a lot. What a lazy, lousy comment. What does it even mean? Places, to my mind, do not produce typical people; they produce individuals with individual stories that may or may not echo a larger story. In the case of L.A., I guess it would be about possibility and space and a kind of (often misguided) hopefulness, and I am happy to identify myself as a product of these qualities. At least sometimes. Why not?"

3.17 "I was shaking, I was so scared," a woman named Angela said. She was dressed in smart casual, the office wear of a businesswoman. Outside, the sky was growing dark as daylight waned. We were seated at a table in a skyscraper robed in glass, on a street I was asked not to divulge, so that Angela could tell me about the time the Federal Bureau of Investigation had freed her from slavery. "My trafficker said, 'Why are you shaking?' I said, 'Because I don't know what's going to happen.'"

She'd been twenty-eight, Angela explained, when a woman brought her to Los Angeles from the Philippines on a lawful visa with the promise of a good job: taking care of old people at a suburban nursing home. What she knew then of L.A. was mainly from TV. "I was so excited. You saw people [on television] living in their own apartments, they can work two or three jobs. That's what I was thinking I could do," Angela said, smiling tightly at me as if it were an instrument of defense. Her trafficker had said the job would be right next to Hollywood, so she'd see movie stars on her days off.

Instead, Angela was driven to Long Beach, where she would be taking care of old people, though for eighteen hours a day, seven days a week, for the next ten years, she was informed. Her passport was taken away. She would have no room of her own, no bed to sleep on. For food, she could eat scraps off the clients' plates. And if she ever tried to escape, her trafficker would get her sent to prison for being in the United States illegally. "When people hear trafficking, they think it's sex trafficking," Angela said. "They haven't heard of labor trafficking. They don't understand."

The city-state was so large, so in flux, with such a vast underclass, it had proved to be an ideal place for enslavers to operate. And Angela was right: though lots of human trafficking was for sex—L.A. was chock-full of brothels and massage parlors—it wasn't only or even mostly about sex. Victims braided hair and made shoes. They washed dishes and watched after people's children. All for little pay, or to pay off a debt, or for no pay at all.

Angela was held in a suburban house in a residential neighborhood. Six elderly people resided in six rooms. For Angela and a man I'll call Robert, another captive, each day began at 4:30 a.m. and ended around 10:00 p.m, no naps allowed. At night they slept in chairs or on the floor. They were expected to wake up every two hours and check on their charges. One client had dementia and roamed at night, Angela explained, so she took to sleeping at the base of the house's front door, to prevent them from leaving. She described an existence of ceaseless exhaustion. Their trafficker lived in the house next door and monitored them constantly. During the day, Angela and Robert often took the clients on a walk. A neighbor noticed that Angela never seemed to have a day off. "I always said, 'Yes, we had one yesterday.' And he said, 'No, I saw you yesterday.'" Angela discouraged such conversations. Her trafficker had threatened that if she ever started talking to the neighbors, or to anyone, she'd be thrown in jail. "And in my country when you say 'jail,' it's scary," Angela said. "It's life or death. You're going to end up beaten up or raped."

One day, Angela was taking out the garbage, and the neighbor came over, reached out to shake her hand and slipped her his phone number. She was petrified. She was allowed to use a phone to text her family, to let them know she was okay, but she wasn't supposed to use it otherwise. She didn't know what to do. How would she ever explain her situation? What if it was a test set up by her trafficker? For days she was transfixed by fear. Gradually it waned. "I guess one day I was just tired of feeling miserable," she said. She dialed the neighbor's number. He answered. "I said, 'Oh, no, no, I'm sorry, I misdialed.'" She quickly hung up. She thought that was the end of it. "But he must've kept my number."

Soon after, Angela said, she received a text message from a woman who identified herself as an FBI agent. Angela was too scared to write back. She was convinced it was her trafficker playing a trick. Weeks passed. Sometimes, when she had a free moment, she'd watch *Law & Order* on one of the clients' TVs; she couldn't imagine law enforcement helping someone like her. "It took me a month," Angela said quietly. "I'm thinking, I'm already in the worst situation. If it's my trafficker, what is she going to do? Is she going to kill me? I guess it's better for her to kill me, because then it's the end. It's over. No more suffering."

She shifted her gaze to address a point in the room somewhere above my left shoulder. Tears filled her eyes. "I can't forget that night," she said. "When I replied, I was on the floor, waiting for [my trafficker] to come, if it was her. But it wasn't. It was the FBI."

3.18 In 1857 the United States Supreme Court heard the case of *Dred Scott v. Sandford*. Scott, an enslaved African American, had sued for his freedom and that of his wife and daughters. The court decided against him, 7–2, arguing that no person of African ancestry was due citizenship in the United States. In the majority opinion Chief Justice Roger Taney wrote that a survey of the nation's laws found that a "perpetual and impassable barrier was intended to be erected between the white race and the one which they had reduced to slavery."

One year prior, Bridget "Biddy" Mason, born into slavery, petitioned a Los Angeles court for her freedom. California law held that any slave in residence was free, but Mason's owner refused. Mason challenged him for her freedom, and Judge Benjamin Hayes sided with her, writing, "And it further appearing by satisfactory proof to the judge here, that all of the said persons of color are entitled to their freedom, and are free and cannot be held in slavery or involuntary servitude, it is therefore argued that they are entitled to their freedom and are free forever."

Later, Mason would buy and sell real estate and become, at her death, one of Los Angeles's wealthiest women, also described as one of its most generous, renowned for her philanthropy. According to Jean K. Williams's *Bridget "Biddy" Mason: From Slave to Businesswoman*, Mason's family quoted her saying, "If you hold your hand closed, nothing good can come of it. The open hand is blessed, for it gives abundance, even as it receives."

3.19 Recently installed in restrooms at LAX were signs saying in multiple languages, "If you or someone you know is being forced to engage in any activity and cannot leave—whether it is commercial sex, housework, farm work, construction, factory, retail, or restaurant work, or any other activity— call the National Human Trafficking Resource Center or the California Coalition to Abolish Slavery and Trafficking (CAST)."

In 2018, CAST received 977 hotline calls. About 42 percent were from community members, 29 percent from potential victims. Kay Buck, CAST's director, said that with so much activity undetected, the true scale of the problem was unknown; anytime law enforcement fought back, slavers adapted. How many massage parlors were staffed by forced labor? How many workers in garment factories were sewing for little pay? CAST was called for as many cases involving labor trafficking as for sex, Buck told me, and they included kids. Recent data found thousands of children enslaved in labor trafficking across the state. One group, brought through LAX from Southeast Asia, were forced to learn martial arts before they arrived so they could pass through immigration more easily by claiming that they were a team visiting the United States for a tournament.

As Angela recalled it, the FBI said that if she wanted to

stay in the country, she needed to help them build a case against her trafficker. "I was [frightened], but I was at a point where I was done. I didn't care anymore. I just wanted to get out." Her face creased. "I wondered, if I stay here, will I wind up killing myself? Will I wind up killing one of my patients?" Tears welled in her eyes again, then were gone.

The FBI extracted Robert first. When Angela's trafficker drove around Long Beach trying to find him, thinking he'd run away, Angela rode shotgun, secretly recording their conversation. "I was so scared. I was wearing the wire and I had my phone, and we were talking in the car, and meanwhile the FBI is texting me, asking if I could adjust the microphone because they couldn't hear!"

"Oh my god!" I exclaimed.

Angela laughed. "In the car I told her, 'I'm sorry but I need to throw up.' We stopped in the middle of the road. I threw up, I was so scared. Because I'm thinking, maybe she knows, and if she knows, maybe she'll kick me out and run me over."

Angela was extracted a week later. A coordinator from CAST drove her to a shelter afterward. That evening would be the first time since she'd arrived in the United States that she slept an entire night without waking up several times, she said. Two years later, her trafficker was sentenced to a prison term of five years. Since then, for Angela, Los Angeles has become home. With CAST's support, she studied, got certified as a nurse's assistant, then took classes on medical billing and coding, which she performed for a dental clinic. "I still get to talk to the patients. I love it," she said, smiling. "I learned I'm still good at taking care of somebody."

It was dark by the time we finished our interview. Through the tower windows, the city-state extended in patchwork—so many overlapping jurisdictions, so many overlapping ideas of home. It looked borderless, yet it was full of borders, self-contained worlds. How many people fell through the cracks each day? Angela mentioned at one point she'd agreed to talk to me because she felt that the more people who heard such stories, the more real human trafficking might seem. It reminded me of something Jacqueline Arellano talked about that day in the desert, near the border: migrants were often spoken about in terms of numbers, as "waves" and "hordes" or other analogies to reduce their individual humanity. Instead, we should use names. We should see faces. "Storytelling is resistance," she said.

4.0 A Black woman from Yuma, Arizona, the youngest of six children, Suzette Shaw studied public health at Arizona State University before moving to the Bay Area, where she would navigate the region's booms and busts for nearly two decades, rising from admin jobs to human resources management. She remembered years full of friends, boyfriends, the occasional wine tasting on the weekend—that '90s dot-com lifestyle that drew so many to Northern California. Then, as bubbles burst, her life slowly began to unravel. She lost a job, gained a job, lost a job. Couch-surfed with friends, then moved in with a sister in Sacramento. She felt like she was spending half her time commuting, crisscrossing Silicon Valley in her car—Mountain View, Palo Alto, South San Francisco. Relationships faded. Her network shrank. Naturally upbeat, quick to smile, Shaw began to feel depressed, and though Prozac helped, she began to experience other things she found disturbing: weight gain, spaciness, the occasional suicidal thought. Some days, Shaw remembered, she felt like she didn't recognize her life anymore, or even who she was as the woman inside it.

She decided to start over: ditch the turmoil of the Valley, return to the familiar Southwest, find a steady job, and save enough money to buy a house. "As a single Black woman, I always said I'd never go back to Yuma," she told me. "But at least I could come back to a safety net." Shaw moved back in with her mother, into the house she left after high school. Soon, old stresses were sharper. Jobs proved scarce. There wasn't enough money to go around. She remembered an uncle trying to shame her into leaving. *You have no husband. No children. You're forty years old, you're a disgrace. Nobody wants you here.* "And that's how I was treated," she said, "before they gave me a one-way ticket to California."

Which is how Shaw came to arrive at Union Station on an overnight train from Yuma—her life stuffed into a duffel bag—and subsequently find herself in Skid Row.

4.1 A thing people didn't often say when describing the city-state was that it was wild, a wilderness, despite being a biodiversity hot spot, a point of thermal anomalies, the only metropolis in the United States split by a mountain range. Los Angeles possesses the country's largest urban national park in the Santa Monica Mountains National Recreation Area. It has Angeles National Forest, forty minutes from Downtown, with more than half a million acres of forests and lakes, several mountains shy of ten thousand feet, and backcountry skiing. "For me it's these rugged hills," the L.A. novelist Percival Everett wrote in *American Desert*. "Hills that defy human occupation. Hills that are not on the way to anywhere."

The archway above Burbank's Saint Finbar Catholic Church reads, THE MOUNTAINS ARE ROUND ABOUT AND THE LORD IS ROUND ABOUT HIS PEOPLE. In 1946, Yvon Chouinard arrived in Burbank at eight years old. A French-speaking child, Chouinard grew up preferring the wild to school, no matter where he found it: hunting rabbits in Griffith Park, diving for lobster off Malibu. "I'd go down to the L.A. River after school and gig frogs," he told me. "I used to swim in the outfall from a movie studio." Chouinard would build his company—later named Patagonia, valued at more than a billion dollars by 2018—from a tin shed located about sixty miles north and west of Burbank, in Ventura, partly because of the high quality of the surfing. The point being, nature proliferates in the city-state and is often intimidating. There are shrub-dense arroyos and coyotes in the street. Once upon a time, the area had been home to megafauna, tusked mammoths. But the wild could also be soft. During a trip in 1959 to her aunt's house in Pasadena, Sylvia Plath counted "pink and red and white oleander bushes, with two avocado trees loaded down with (alas) not-yet-ripe fruit, a peach tree, a guava tree, a persimmon tree, a fig tree and others"—and the list might be so much longer: the manzanita, the buckthorn, the jacaranda that bloom in May all lavender and gaudy like amateur beauty queens. Reyner Banham wrote in *Los Angeles: The Architecture of Four Ecologies* (1971), "Whatever man has done subsequently to the climate and environment of Southern California, it remains one of the ecological wonders of the habitable world."

Still, there was a good reason why the city-state wasn't known for nature, precisely because of what man had done: built a concrete kingdom. A study by the architecture studio Woods Bagot found more cement in L.A. County dedicated to surface parking—some 101 square miles—than what would be needed for an area the size of four Manhattans. Much of the county simply roasted under the sun. Poorer neighborhoods were frequently labeled "heat islands," lacking shade or parks, where the sky was never sheltering, the palm trees useless when it came to blocking light. L.A.'s palms, in fact, were an imported plant, installed mainly for appearance's sake, to make the region look more like the French Riviera—and if a visitor ever thought of Los Angeles as obsessed with image, uncaring about its worst-off, here was a symbol for easy confirmation.

But the city-state was perhaps harshest for one group: the tens of thousands of citizens who lived by wilderness rules and struggled to survive, sleeping in tents and cars, garages and cheap motels, those people known as "homeless," "facing homelessness," or "residence-challenged," or by meaner spirits as "bums," "vagrants," and "the walking dead." As of 2020, with more than sixty-five thousand people unhoused, Los Angeles County was the epicenter of homelessness in the United States, and the homeless were those who had it worst. People who scavenged for food and snuck water from garden spigots. Who struggled with the worst of the "wicked city"—drug addiction, mental illness, men threatening to crack their heads with baseball bats. A *Kaiser Health News* analysis of recent medical-examiner data found that life expectancy for a homeless woman in Los Angeles was forty-eight.

And in response, officials vowed to build housing and mostly failed. Volunteers, charities, outreach workers struggled valiantly, and the homeless population expanded. In 2019 the county managed to get almost twenty-three thousand people into housing, according to the L.A. Homeless Services Authority, and still the problem grew. The crisis had sixty-thousand-plus faces. The solution had none.

At a packed public meeting at the Philosophical Research Society in Los Feliz, a speaker made a comment about a "street person," and a woman shouted from the back, "You mean 'a wilderness person'!" Our homeless problem, also called the housing problem, also our problem with mental health, was the city-state's great catastrophe. It looked to have no end. And nowhere was it rougher than in Skid Row.

4.2 As an actual neighborhood of Los Angeles, Skid Row has different sections and separate communities. Its homeless citizens range from homesteaders to transients. The district occupies some fifty blocks downtown, east of Main, south of Third, west of Alameda, north of Seventh. It can be easy to wander into; the shift from surrounding blocks isn't always clear, when not too far away are tourist attractions such as The Broad museum, Frank Gehry's billowing Disney Hall, other works by the billionaire Eli Broad, the city-state's Lorenzo de' Medici of late. In Downtown generally it's not unusual for sidewalks to be full of men and women in business suits walking to lunch, and men and women in shower sandals pushing one another around in wheelchairs.

A district of the poor since the 1930s, Skid Row's history has been mostly one of demolition: the demolition of boardinghouses, low-cost hotels, and inexpensive housing stock; the demolition of the hopes of those who might build affordable public housing units. It also had a history, counterintuitively, of people fighting to "keep Skid Row scary," as the political scientist Virginia Eubanks noted in *Automating Inequality* (2018), the idea being to preserve Skid Row as a containment zone, concentrated with services and caseworkers. In fact, one recent threat to residents came from a new generation of Angelenos who didn't mind living nearby, their Downtown existence made pleasantly grittier by a little edge (a homeless woman muttering to herself), as long as it wasn't too gritty (a homeless man pissing on their doorstep). One new condo building advertised "Gritty Is Pretty" in its marketing materials. A map provided to inquiring applicants highlighted wine bars and coffee roasters, and failed to mention Skid Row even once—a map to a future version of Los Angeles, where the neighborhood had been all but erased.

Was it surprising that people who lived elsewhere in the city-state often said someone lived "on" Skid Row, rather than "in" it?

Was it a shock when authorities raided encampments and called their operation a "clean-up" or "sweep," as if the people and their belongings were so much trash to be brushed away?

Many of those brushed-away people would be Black, it needs to be said. Of more than sixty-six thousand people experiencing homelessness, Black people made up 34 percent; in the same period, African Americans represented only about 8 percent of the county's population. That disparity reflected a national problem: according to reports, Black Americans represented about 13 percent of the United States' general population but 40 percent of its homeless populace. A 2019 report from the Los Angeles Homeless Services Authority took care to note, "The impact of institutional and structural racism in education, criminal justice, housing, employment, health care, and access to opportunities cannot be denied: homelessness is a by-product of racism in America."

Steps from the garment district, Skid Row is a zone of mostly low-rise buildings, blocks lined with convenience stores and wholesalers. The light is like anywhere else, blue and gold and drowsy. Roots from old trees often break up the sidewalk, then, closer in, those sidewalks begin to fill with tents and tarps. Still, this looked like most of the city-state at the time. Skid Row provides refuge to thousands of people in supportive housing, in mission or shelter beds, or sleeping outdoors. Some encampments would be tidy, with a broom propped against a wall, a tub of OxiClean beside a bucket. Other setups were shaggier—broken glass, discarded mattresses, rats scurrying around. Deeper in, sidewalks were often full, impassable. "I think it's on a scale I hadn't anticipated, block after block of people," a United Nations monitor on extreme poverty said after touring the neighborhood. "When you see how concentrated it is, it's more shocking."

"Poverty is personal," the poet Luis Alberto Urrea wrote in *Across the Wire*. "It smells and it shocks and it invades your space."

Suzette Shaw walked me around Skid Row on a bright September morning. When she first arrived, in 2012, the neighborhood had been a shock. She'd never seen anyone get high before. She'd never been so tormented by men. She remembered her first day, San Pedro Street, a guy lingering outside a clinic, talking like it was his job to harass any women coming and going. "I'm a woman out here in the world on my own," she recalled telling herself. "There's truly no one looking out. You have to fend for yourself."

For two years Shaw moved between transitional hotels or stayed at the Downtown Women's Center, trying to put her life together. Living became an intensely lonely experience, she recalled. She was afraid to walk around. She frequently got lost. She described an atmosphere of near-constant menace—a man stalking her for months; a man threatening her with a gun while she was waiting in line to eat. Skid Row tends to be a male space and a predatory one. Women are frequently attacked and raped. While trying to get her own foothold, Shaw started an empowerment group to help other women on the street, funding it with her EBT card, paying each week for coffee, fresh fruit, a box of pastries—she knew about organization, and she wanted to help. But she also needed to help herself. "I can articulate this now," Shaw told me, "but back then I didn't have the words, the understanding. I was dealing with a lot of mental health challenges then that had built up over time, where I'd ended up at this stage in the middle part of my life." The toll had built gradually, she said, from losing her job, her home, having no place to go, but the effects were daily. Fear, disgrace, anxiety. Frequent crying, constant distress. Nevertheless, she kept pushing. One book that helped, Shaw said, was *The Body Keeps the Score: Brain, Mind, and Body in the Healing of Trauma*, by Bessel van der Kolk. "Neuroscience research shows that very few psychological problems are the result of defects in understanding; most originate in pressures from deeper regions in the brain that drive our perception and attention," van der Kolk wrote. "When the alarm bell of the emotional brain keeps signaling that you are in danger, no amount of insight will silence it."

Taking me around Skid Row a few months before the coronavirus pandemic, Shaw hugged and high-fived residents who recognized her. She was a local success. Back on her feet, renting an apartment nearby, at fifty-six she had become a well-known advocate, spokeswoman, and activist-poetess, also a frequent presence on county committees, fighting specifically for Black women's health. By the time we met, she had lived in or near Skid Row for more than seven years. It was a living community, she emphasized, not a containment zone. "Rich white people come down here, look around, and ask, 'How the hell can people live like this?'" she said. "I tell them, 'Just as people become conditioned to Beverly Hills, people become conditioned to this.'" One man we met, who didn't want to be named, told me, "Everybody sees us as vermin, as roaches, as something to get rid of. It's dehumanizing." Everybody who? "Everybody," he stressed. "Police. The city. You."

"We have to talk about who people are rather than pathologizing them," Shaw said. "I'm a Black woman living in Skid Row. I'm a Black woman, period. My advocacy was birthed from pain, but people don't like to talk about pain, the perseverance through the pain. That would be giving me too much credit."

4.3 "We found ourselves driving down narrow, dimly lit side streets, where we saw hundreds of homeless people, refugees of economic and social disenfranchisement, darkened silhouettes seeking respite from the chill of winter cold along the greasy pavement. It was a haunting déjà-vu moment: our families experienced this 166 years ago" (Cindi Moar Alvitre, descendant of the Tongva, *LAtitudes: An Angeleno's Atlas*).

4.4 Living on the edge of Hollywood, Rachel and I became habituated to a man collapsed behind our gate. A pool of diarrhea on the doorstep. Narcotics confetti on the sidewalk—singed foil, needle caps—and people openly shooting up on the corner. Men so high they'd prop themselves against parking signs and pass out, still standing. The southern end of our street got so gnarly with encampments, drugs, and violence, the newspaper did a three-part investigation, and the problem still felt underreported.

One winter morning, at sunrise, I found a man near our front door, huddled over a campfire he'd built from our garbage.

I hated it, despaired about it, and sometimes tried not to see it. Conflicting feelings boiled inside me every day. Anger, shame, guilt. Frustration, disassociation, fatigue. I gave money to the local food bank and nonprofits. I said hello during walks and handed out water. I also wanted my fucking sidewalk back. Feelings got raw on the block— reactionary, furious—whether toward NIMBY (Not In My Backyard) property owners, two-faced city officials, or the methy-looking white guy who told our neighbor exactly how he intended to rape her. In a newspaper interview, the mayor admitted that he was often woken up by someone rooting through his trash cans—and he lived in Hancock Park, one of the best-preserved wealthy enclaves. "A friend of mine was held at knifepoint a couple days ago," he admitted. "This can't continue."

It continued. It continued worsening.

A lot of the time I just wanted the problem to go away.

4.5 Expelling undesirables was a long-standing fantasy in the city-state. In the 1850s, during the years of gold fever, the *Los Angeles Star* demanded, "Cannot some plan be devised to remove [Native people] from our midst? Could they not be removed to a plantation in the vicinity of our city, and put under the control of an overseer?" In 1983, prior to the Summer Olympics, a city councilman suggested shipping the homeless population to a farm thirty miles north of Downtown—"Let them sweat it out in the sun, grow vegetables to eat, and learn a trade"—as if obeying the ostensible logic predicted by George Orwell in *Down and Out in Paris and London* (1933): "For the question is, what to do with men who are underfed and idle; and the answer—to make them grow their own food—imposes itself automatically." But the impulse seemed less common sense, more sinisterly paternalistic. More like when Jack London posed, back in 1902, as a destitute sailor in "the Abyss," London's version of Skid Row at the time. "Day by day I become convinced that not only is it unwise, but it is criminal for the people of the Abyss to marry," London wrote. "They are the stones by the builder rejected. There is no place for them in the social fabric, while all the forces of society drive them downward till they perish."

More recently, at a 2018 meeting for residents of Sherman Oaks to learn about housing initiatives, protesters shut down the conversation, shouting "No common sense!" One of them proposed detaining Los Angeles's homeless population in the desert, out of sight. "When we interned the Japanese during the Second World War, we didn't intern them in the city," the man fumed.

Bill Shishima, born in Los Angeles, grew up near Skid Row, though he didn't experience homelessness until the government incarcerated him and his family for three years in one of the concentration camps—as President Roosevelt called them at the time—constructed to imprison 120,000 Japanese American citizens thanks to 1942's Executive Order 9066, naming Americans of Japanese descent a "hostile and enemy race."

Shishima was in sixth grade when he and his family were bused to Heart Mountain in Park County, Wyoming. Like nearly all of the incarcerated, Shishima had done nothing wrong except not be white. In the camp, he was given an identification number, 17866D, and his family was assigned to a barracks. The climate was subzero in winter, blazing in summer, he remembered. He credited his survival in part to his experiences in Boy Scouts. Oddly enough, there were so many children in the camp who'd been scouts at home, they needed to form seven troops. "Scouting is what kept us alive," he recalled.

Order 9066 began, "Whereas the successful prosecution of the war requires every possible protection against espionage and against sabotage . . ." And yet, a great majority of Japanese Americans at the time pledged loyalty to the United States—"a remarkable, even extraordinary degree of loyalty," according to the Munson Report, a 1940 study commissioned to measure sentiment. Still, the United States had a long record of anti-Asian behavior. The attack on Pearl Harbor fostered suspicion that citizens with Japanese heritage were spies. "I'm for catching every Japanese in America, Alaska and Hawaii now and putting them in concentration camps," Congressman John Rankin said in December 1941. The managing secretary of the Salinas Vegetable Grower-Shipper Association was quoted in May 1942 in *The Saturday Evening Post*: "We're charged with wanting to get rid of the Japs for selfish reasons. We might as well be honest. We do. It's a question of whether the white man lives on the Pacific Coast or the brown men." Finding similar quotes from the period wasn't difficult. From an editorial in the *Los Angeles Times*, April 22, 1943: "As a race, the Japanese have made for themselves a record of conscienceless treachery unsurpassed in history." It felt like dipping into what the local poet Sesshu Foster dubbed, in his collection *City of the Future*, the "apartheid imagination." "The apartheid imagination requires no location, no physical body; because it has laws, records, court buildings, cells, conversations and life."

The apartheid imagination:

Enabled people not to think much.

Enabled people who looked like me to rip people who didn't look like me out of their homes and drop them down dark holes.

Enabled people to treat other people like garbage.

When we first met, Shishima and I initially bonded after discovering we were both Eagle Scouts, and he agreed to tour me through the Japanese American National Museum in Downtown's Little Tokyo, where one of the actual barracks from Heart Mountain had been restored and installed. Shishima pointed at the wooden slats. The first winter, he said, temperatures fell as low as thirty below zero. Wind would whip through the uninsulated walls. "Some people had to make their own mattresses," he recalled. "Initially they made them out of straw. It didn't smell too good."

As we talked that afternoon, the United States was busy removing migrant children from their parents, incarcerating them in conditions some compared to concentration camps. Children who, in many cases, were sent to "sponsor" homes elsewhere in the country while their parents' cases were being weighed, though the government, apparently less capable of record-keeping than during World War II, was reported to be frequently unknowing of which children—numbering in the thousands, according to the Associated Press—it had taken from which parents. And it claimed that any effort to unite them again might be too difficult to be worth the effort, also stating, for good measure, that to remove a child from their new "home" in order to rejoin them with their parents "would present grave child welfare concerns." "It would destabilize the permanency of their existing home environment, and could be traumatic to the children," an official said.

Shishima said that such historical echoes, however unreal they seemed, were why he often struck up conversations with museum visitors. "You can read about it, but if you hear it firsthand, I think it's more meaningful," he told me. "I was *there*. I was *incarcerated*. It makes a difference." Eventually the federal government paid reparations to the Japanese Americans who had been incarcerated and their heirs, something long overdue but still seemingly unlikely for Black Americans, Shishima pointed out. I wanted to know, did people think of his story as a Los Angeles story or one about the United States? Neither, he said. People thought it was a Japanese story, or a Japanese American story, no matter that the perpetrators and victims were all Americans. To this day, occasionally people asked why he spoke English so well. "I've heard people on the street tell me, 'Go back where you came from!' I say, 'But I'm from Los Angeles.'"

4.6 In 1991, on the fiftieth anniversary of the attack on Pearl Harbor, President George H. W. Bush said, "The internment of Americans of Japanese ancestry was a great injustice, and it will never be repeated." Of course, history repeats itself constantly. Less than a year from the day I spent with Shishima, news broke that the federal government was proposing to set up a detention center for migrant children at Oklahoma's Fort Sill; it had previously housed more than one thousand people in 2014. Before that, in 1942, it was also one of the camps holding Japanese Americans.

"Past, present, and future are incompatible determinations . . . But every event has them all," the philosopher J. M. E. McTaggart wrote in *The Nature of Existence* (1921). Suggesting that time was unreal, a paradox. If something happened way back when, it had also existed in the present moment for a period. Therefore, it had also been something to anticipate in days ahead. Meaning, any event that hadn't happened yet would soon be present and past, too. But the past, the present, and the future were supposed to be exclusive from one another. After all, the present was the only place where we lived.

Though perhaps not in the United States.

Definitely not in Los Angeles.

4.7 "History in Los Angeles is not chronological," Dan Johnson said flatly, approximately one minute into our first conversation. Originally from Virginia, a son of the U.S. Navy, for most of the last decade Johnson had lived in "Skidrokyo"— the quarter between Skid Row and Little Tokyo—as a man of multiple occupations: reviewing restaurants, scouting film locations, producing radio segments for the Dodgers. He'd also worked with homeless men at the Midnight Mission for several years, helping to improve their reading skills, using *The Skid Row Reader*, a textbook he put together himself.

We met one summer afternoon near the bong souk—it wasn't called that, but it should be—east of the Historic Quarter downtown, where every window display was full of glass pipes. Johnson had the look of an outlaw from a spaghetti western—droopy mustache, sad eyes—and tended to speak in paragraphs lacking much in the way of stopping points. "History in Los Angeles is not chronological," he repeated, staring across the street, "and to understand Los Angeles you need to grasp that its history is simultaneous, a pastiche, full of waves of innovation and backsliding, with people working through their own independent narratives in a chaotic fashion, where all of us live under the shadow of all these different stories, plus a giant body of sadness that will never be accounted for, that memory will not recollect, a sadness that the historical record will not show when it comes time to account for this city of conquest, imprisonment, and ambition, where people have been quietly destroying themselves and each other since the 1700s"—he took a breath—"and yeah, maybe the same can be said of other American cities, but here it's cut with the idea 'I can go to Los Angeles and become a star,' where a man or a woman can show up and go look at the big houses in the Palisades, the big Victorians in Echo Park, and said man or woman can realistically think 'I'm going to make it,' but imagine you start out or arrive here thinking 'I'm going to make it' and then thirty years later you don't, maybe instead of the mansion you wanted, instead of the tower with the swimming pool on the roof, you wind up in low-income housing or worse"—another breath—"because that's the shit that destroys the egos of people here perhaps more than anything else, newcomers and natives, and frankly it's a condition all but omnipresent that few people speak about: the disparity of what you want when you arrive in Los Angeles, the things you assume you'll get along the way, and then the reality of the situation when it doesn't work out.

"History in Los Angeles isn't chronological," he said

again, still staring across the street. "It's coinciding, ever-present, and constantly fucking people up."

Around Skid Row, some blocks look more doomsday than others. The vicinity of the Midnight Mission is often where things seem worst. A woman in a bra and underwear slumped over a chair. An angry man walking around with his genitals exposed. But also to be seen were many people assisting others. Residents helped one another move belongings. People shared food in the sunlight. Nearby were shelters, clinics, employment agencies. A long line waited for two guys giving free haircuts under a pop-up tent. Later, asked if he ever got used to it, Johnson shook his head, both yes and no. "I might be numb at this point," he said. "I've spent so much time aggressively loving and advocating for Los Angeles and also bitterly hating it. Really, really hating it."

The Midnight Mission, operating since 1914, was one of Skid Row's oldest social service organizations. Johnson's class took place in a brightly lit room full of computers. His homemade textbook included some two dozen short readings that he used to start discussion; in his opinion, adult education worked best when it encouraged people to ramble meaningfully. "I tell people it's a digressive text. It's a digressive class," he said. "We spent twenty minutes the other day talking shit on Drake."

That day, five men showed up: white, Black, Latino, ranging in age from teenager to senior. Johnson asked everyone to turn to an excerpt from John Fante's *Ask the Dust*. Honestly, it felt like a setup—the day I was visiting, he picked *the* L.A. novel?—but Johnson insisted that the choice belonged to Ben, an older white guy with a thick beard and a crisp Lakers T-shirt. Published in 1939, *Ask the Dust* came out the same year as two other local classics,

The Day of the Locust by Nathanael West and Raymond Chandler's *The Big Sleep*. The main character in *Dust*, Arturo Bandini, was a wannabe writer with a stomach rotting from eating too many oranges—oranges being the source of L.A.'s booming at the time—who wandered Downtown thinking of all the ways he'd been wronged. The men in class took turns reading aloud. Johnson would interrupt to discuss tricky words or ask questions. An older gentleman, Arthur, read slowly, "'And I remembered what Helen wore that day—a white dress, and how it made me sing at the loins when I touched it.'"

"Arthur, what are your loins?" Johnson asked.

"Your clothes?" Arthur offered.

"Your sneakers?" said someone else.

"No, no. Your goods, man," Johnson said. "The package. If you're singing in the loins, if you see a nice-looking chick, what could it mean, Arthur?"

Arthur laughed. "He's getting turned on!"

The men giggled together, bashfully. Arthur said under his breath, "This guy's singing in the loins constantly." Later, during a discussion about brothels, one of the men likened the days of red-light districts to today's Skid Row, where vice was tolerated as long as it didn't creep out into, say, Bel Air. "It's like when the cops drive around, and you've got folks smoking crack, selling heroin, and the cops drive by and don't do shit about it," the man said. "They know where they're at and they know what they're doing."

After class, Ben, the man who picked the day's reading, told me he'd been in and out of the Mission for several years. He liked *Ask the Dust* because Bandini was whacked-out not on opioids but visions, dreams of things that should've happened for him. "So many of the guys coming in here, they've been gone so long they're seeing stuff that's not there," he said. "They'll be talking, saying stuff they're seeing, and we don't see what they're seeing. There's a lot of great storytellers on the smoke deck, you better believe."

Ben picked up the textbook and tapped the pages. "[Bandini is] making stuff up to keep himself going. That's why this is my favorite story. I can identify with it. He knows he's losing it, he's going downhill, but he's trying to stay alive. That could be me."

4.8 "The people of Los Angeles, then as now, deal less day to day with geologic or climactic time than with human time," William Deverell wrote in *Whitewashed Adobe: The Rise of Los Angeles and the Remaking of Its Mexican Past.* "And human time has many a memory blind spot."

4.9 About a week after Johnson's class, two older white men in sunglasses stood outside a tennis court in Griffith Park.

"Everyone thinks the landlord's made out of millions," the first one said.

"You take care of your properties because you care about them," the other said.

"These people are animals, they ruin everything, renters. You know what their problem is?"

"What's their problem?"

"Envy," the first one said. "They're envious. If they'd worked hard their whole lives, if they worked like us, they'd own property. Evelyn, my wife, she overheard one lady who didn't know I was the landlord, Evelyn says this lady wanted revenge against her landlord over something, so she runs the water all night so the utility bills go up. Can you believe that shit? The selfish bitch. Everyone thinks the landlord's a millionaire."

"I'll tell you the only solution for that."

"What's that?"

"Go out, buy an AK-47, unload a full magazine into the bitch."

"That's what you'd do?"

"It relieves the stress."

"I wish. I'll tell you something about envy. The first Porsche I ever bought, someone ripped the goddamn emblem off. First week, tore the goddamn thing off. Who the hell does that? Pure envy, these people. Now if they'd done something with their lives, worked hard, worked like we did—I mean, why the fuck you gotta go piss on a brand-new Porsche?"

"So, you going to the club?"

"Yeah, let's go relax."

4.10 In 1966, daily life for Merilee Farrier meant a lot of driving. She'd start by piloting the family RV from Downtown to Burbank, to drop off her husband at his factory job, then to El Monte to leave their baby with her mother. Next she drove to West Covina where she worked in a department store, then, at the end of the day, she'd reverse the commute, grabbing infant and husband before they'd park the RV in a lot downtown, eat dinner as a family, and spend the night. The loop required 128 miles of driving, ten gallons of gas. Before, the family had lived in a house, but financial straits led to living out of a motor home. "We've really begun to feel that the freeways, particularly the Hollywood Freeway, which is a beautiful road, belong to us," Farrier's husband said in an interview with *Cry California*, an environmental magazine at the time, which first reported their story. "It's not the same feeling you get about a house and a lot, of course, but it's definitely a sense of ownership."

When the article came out, reporters from other publications started calling. They wanted to interview the Farriers. It seemed ludicrous that a family needed to live out of their car. Unfortunately, *Cry California*'s editor said that any further conversations with the Farriers would be impossible. The magazine had made them up. They were a hoax, a wild fantasy. "I thought it was obvious," the editor later told *The New York Times*.

As of 2019, fifty-something years later, more than sixteen thousand people lived full-time in cars, vans, or RVs, according to the Greater Los Angeles Homeless Count. The same year, the *Santa Monica Daily Press* coined the term *vanlords* for a special class of lessor: people who rented out parked vehicles, at about $300 a month, for other people to sleep in at night—vehicles that didn't even run, that turned into temporary hostels, parked on the Westside in front of million-dollar homes. VAN LIFE IS NOT A CRIME read the bumper stickers. "Bottom line, being homeless requires people to do sketchy things to get shelter and sleep," one tenant said. "Without those, it's hard to keep it together."

4.11 Another piece of local vocabulary is the "first flush." The first flush was the moment in the city-state's calendar when, after months of drought, dark clouds finally arrived in the late autumn and the rain fell in torrents, shoveling all the garbage lying around into the ocean, turning the beaches into dumps of lawn fertilizer, lawn ornaments, and lawn chairs. Basically, each fall and winter, when the rain finally arrived, the vast, dusty bowl of L.A. tipped toward the Pacific, and anything unmoored ran through the storm drain system, out to the Santa Monica and San Pedro Bays. As a result, the Los Angeles River, sometimes just a smear of water, would be so blanketed with moving garbage it was difficult to spot patches of non-trash—the reason why local swimmers and surfers were warned to wait three days after a storm before entering the ocean, and those who refused sometimes caught giardiasis or something worse.

The local environmental scientists Marcus Eriksen and Anna Cummins, a husband-and-wife team who lived in Mid City, explained all of this one afternoon in their kitchen. One year, Eriksen said, he had watched the "flush" run by from the banks of Ballona Creek, and the garbage was so dense, so metaphorically smoglike, as to be uncountable. "Bottle, bottle, bag, cup, Styrofoam container, Styrofoam plate—"

"And here's a piece blowing in from the street," Cummins said as a plastic shopping bag blew in through their kitchen door.

A 2001 study by the Brookings Institution, "Sprawl Hits the Wall," found that residents of the city-state consumed about twenty-five acres of the world's natural resources each year. That was 38 percent higher than the United States' per capita average, and more than four times that of the world. "Put another way, the 'ecological footprint' of Los Angeles is approximately equal to the size of California, Arizona, New Mexico, and Texas combined," the authors wrote. In 2009 Eriksen and Cummins cofounded the 5 Gyres Institute, a nonprofit that fights plastic pollution. Eriksen's activism started during the Gulf War. "If you saw the burning oil wells that Saddam set on fire before they left Kuwait . . . I was one of the marines on the ground, sitting in a foxhole," he said. "The whole time I'm thinking, 'This is insane. We've come to rescue a tiny country, one of the richest in the world, because of what's underground.'" Eriksen and the marine next to him, both originally from Louisiana, promised themselves that if they ever got home, they'd build a raft like Huckleberry Finn and float down the Mississippi River. It was a fantasy to distract themselves, but after the war Eriksen couldn't shake it. In 2003 he built a raft with two-hundred-plus soda bottles and spent five months on the Mississippi. He spotted plastic everywhere. In 2008 he sailed two thousand miles from Los Angeles to Hawaii on another recycled ship, fifteen thousand bottles this time, with thirty old sailboat masts lashed together for a deck, and found even more pollution: microscopic debris permeating the water, even in the fish he caught to eat. He wrote in his expedition diary, "The entrails and stomach are spread over the wooden cutting board. The stomach, roughly the size of an almond, feels hard, unlike the stomachs of other fish I've dissected to examine gut contents. I touch it with the edge of the filet knife and it splits open. Seventeen fragments of plastic pour out. There's nothing else inside. It was filled to capacity."

A few months before the beginning of World War II, Aldous Huxley strolled a beach "some fifteen or twenty miles southwest of Los Angeles" with Thomas Mann and their wives, only to come upon condoms, endless condoms, as far as their eyes could see. "The scale was American, the figures astronomical. Ten million saw I at a glance. Ten million emblems and mementoes of Modern Love."

A major contributing factor to our waste, in Eriksen and

Cummins's estimation, was consumerism's shift after World War II from circular to linear thinking, from preferring goods meant to last to products designed to fail. It was the concept of planned obsolescence: where people once took pride in owning durable things, now they favored buying stuff—clothes, technology—that would break quickly or become unfashionable, so they could purchase more. And of the nearly seven billion tons of plastic waste humans had created and tossed away, almost all of it would live practically forever, much of it in the oceans, discarded as if we'd never see it again.

One day in the springtime, Patagonia, Yvon Chouinard's company and one of 5 Gyre's corporate sponsors, invited me to join Eriksen and Cummins on a boat to see what plastics could be found in nearby waters. We sailed from a small marina in Santa Barbara. The surface was barely rumbled. Eriksen and Cummins dropped a trawling device behind the boat that looked like an anchor wearing a long sock— the same method they'd used to sample patches of ocean around the globe. After an hour, up came the trawler, and inside were seaweed, jellies, small stones, and then shards of plastic, from a long, thin ribbon to pieces as small as confetti. That afternoon, headed back to the marina, Eriksen unwrapped a treat he'd brought home from Dubai, as big as several bowling balls: the densely compacted contents of a dead camel's stomach, about forty pounds' worth of plastic bags. It reminded me of the afternoon I spent at their house, when Eriksen had taken me to their garage to show off a cross section of urban life he'd obtained in New York City: a large piece of turf from Dead Horse Bay, an open-pit landfill that had been used at one point to render carcasses from a nearby glue factory. Closed in the 1950s, the landfill had been planted over, but when Eriksen visited, the ocean was tearing it apart. Different layers looked like stripes of eras of consumer plastics: horse bones at the bottom and then strata upon strata of panty hose, plastic toys, plastic deodorant casings, all nearly intact. "Planned obsolescence is just so much more profitable," Eriksen said to himself almost admiringly.

In an article in 2004, the urban historian Dolores Hayden noted that Harley Earl, an early head of design at General Motors, had promoted exaggerated tail fins on vehicles because he wanted customers to desire the new, the trendy, the flashy, to signify their status. He called it "dynamic obsolescence," and now, as a result, Hayden wrote, "old cars fill junkyards as new cars sit in gridlock. Old neighborhoods decline as new ones echo with the sounds of hammers. But what about the residents?"

4.12 During random visits to Skid Row, "planned obsolescence" would pop up in my thoughts, as if Skid Row were a precinct the city-state had set aside, as many citizens had fantasized over the years, for people to disappear or be disappeared. A place where, at the same time, politicians rode through unclothed, wearing dehydrated bullshit hung like sausages from their ears, because their pronouncements weren't worth much more than that.

Anytime I went around Skid Row, I hated it, all the suffering, the filth. It ignited my anger, definitely my shame. "You can't write a story about L.A. that doesn't turn around in the middle or get lost" (Eve Babitz, *Slow Days, Fast*

Company). Truthfully, the city-state's homeless problem had slowly cauterized my nerve endings—each time I ran to the door because a woman outside was screaming, or found a man sleeping in the shadow of my car. And still I could be shocked. Suitcase Joe, the nom de plume of a street photographer who worked around Skid Row, once texted me a picture he said he couldn't bring himself to publish: a young Black man lying dead in the street, naked but for his socks, unattended in broad daylight.

I saw it on my phone and started crying.

I hated it, I hate it, I will hate it.

None of it proved that Los Angeles needed to be this way.

4.13 As of 2020, around 80 percent of children enrolled in the Los Angeles Unified School District lived below the poverty line. The head of St. John's Well Child and Family Center, a nonprofit medical center treating low-income residents in South Central, told the newspaper, "We pull cockroaches out of kids' ears every week."

At Nuffer Elementary, in Norwalk, about a dozen miles from Downtown, a report in 2018 found that at some point during the previous year, 154 of the school's 328 students had lived in a car, motel, homeless shelter, or temporarily with friends or family. "We call them headwinds: things that are blowing in the students' faces that prevent them from learning," Makara Kar, Nuffer's principal, told me. Kar said that his school ran a number of programs to help. In one, they gave out backpacks on Mondays containing up to thirty pounds of food. He'd had one family getting three backpacks a week, all for six people living in a single bedroom. Then the parents told him they were moving to another school district, though for happy reasons; living off the donated food, the parents had saved and saved and finally could afford a place of their own.

But not all children had families or knew their parents. The RightWay Foundation, a nonprofit in Crenshaw, provided mental health and employment services for foster youth, particularly those who'd had it rougher. "The youth we serve are predominately African American, ages eighteen to twenty-five," said Franco Vega, RightWay's executive director. "Many have been through multiple changes in foster care placements and are working through early traumatic experiences that occurred prior to and during their time in foster care." On a stormy November morning, a dozen or so young people sat at long tables in RightWay's offices in the Baldwin Hills Crenshaw Plaza shopping mall. They were engaged in a weeklong program to help them land jobs or internships in the arts. Some traveled more than two hours on different buses each morning to be there. One young woman told me she was homeless, hustling to pay her bills. One guy showed up dripping wet and shivering because he didn't have a jacket. (Someone made a telephone call to line one up.)

The city-state has the United States' largest population of foster youth. The first time we spoke, Vega recited grim statistics: foster youth were twice as likely to experience PTSD as war veterans. Soon after leaving the system, half were unemployed, a quarter incarcerated, and more than a third would be homeless after eighteen months. Generally, RightWay's clientele had been failed by the system in multiple ways, Vega said, and possessed backgrounds of complex trauma. They struggled with setting goals, struggled with relationships. "We're the safety net that they need," he said.

One of the young men, Carlos, wore a blue Dodger cap and a hoodie. In his early twenties, he looked sixteen, baby-faced, with a thin goatee. Carlos was recently out of jail and wanted to be a chef. "My mom told me that she finally sees her son," he said. "For like five-plus years I was doped out. Carrying guns, drugs, running the streets. She didn't know who I was. She was scared of me. Now she sees me coming out of prison, doing good. She says that she sees peace despite the fact I lost my dad this year, despite that I lost people last year. Knowing that all this stuff keeps happening, and here I am holding my composure, trying to fix myself first before I do anything else."

To hear his mother say such things, Carlos explained, meant the world to him. Their relationship had been rough, and he still struggled to understand why she'd given him up—him, his younger brother, and his older sister—but he tried not to hold it against her, even if he didn't quite know why she was the way she was. He choked up a little and spread his mustache with two fingers. "I'm learning to be patient with myself and with her."

Above the mall, the sky thundered. The young people practiced interviewing skills and worked on their résumés. Carlos's voice sounded like other voices I heard that day: a SoCal monotone, the same timbre to describe a meal at Jack in the Box or the night you watched your friend get shot, as if to render trivial events and tragic ones in an equally manageable form of consequential.

Carlos said offhandedly at one point that his immediate

focus was trying to fix his housing situation. There was a good chance he'd be homeless in two days, and he didn't know what to do. Vega promised they'd find a way to fix that.

4.14 "The federal government could render homelessness rare, brief and nonrecurring. The cure for homelessness is housing, and, as it happens, the money is available: Congress could shift billions in annual federal subsidies from rich homeowners to people who don't have homes" (Binyamin Appelbaum, *The New York Times*).

"Here is a city where we've dreamt brilliantly of virtue while doing spectacularly unvirtuous things. It practically vibrates with brilliant denial in the service of spectacular yearning, self-interest, and material indulgence" (Jenny Price, "Thirteen Ways of Seeing Nature in LA").

4.15 In 2013, Nathan Deuel and his wife, both surfers, purchased what he described as the last house in Venice that sold for under a million bucks. A bungalow on Sunset Avenue, two blocks from the ocean, the house was in bad need of repair and faced a noisy neighbor: an active bus depot. Klieg lights would flip on in the early morning and flood their bedroom windows while hundreds of Metro buses roared to life, backing up—*beep beep beep*—before heading off to pick up commuters. So they bought blackout curtains and a noise machine, and Deuel started telling himself a story, the same one he told their six-year-old daughter, that maybe they could reframe how they thought of their raucous neighbor— to consider the aggravation not a tax but a source of pride because they got to play a role, however passively, in the city-state's gearbox. "I even believed my story, at least during the day," he said. "Cars were awful! Buses were great! And they had to park somewhere."

Then, one morning, the buses were gone. Years went by, and the lot remained empty; people speculated that Google had bought the lot to erect a campus. Gradually a tent city appeared. Trash piled up, but this wasn't a surprise: at that point Venice still expressed pride in being rough, despite recent gentrification brought by tech companies and yuppies (MAKE VENICE SHIT AGAIN said locally sold hats). Also, not far from Deuel's block was "Skid Rose," a portion of Rose Avenue known for open-air drug dealing, petty crime, an ambience of lawlessness. Then news came in 2018 that the former depot would become a homeless shelter, part of the city's "A Bridge Home" program. Many people protested. Others, like Deuel's family, were supportive, if quiet about it. "You couldn't walk around without one of your neighbors screaming it's going to ruin the neighborhood," he explained. "Or someone whispering in your ear they think it's a good thing."

As much as anything, Deuel said, his opinion about the shelter was influenced by his daughter's reaction. It had been five years since they'd arrived, but seeing people sleeping on the sidewalk still pained her. She had believed his story about valuing the buses, and wouldn't a homeless shelter play an even more important role? In November 2018 Deuel published an op-ed in the newspaper, "How I Learned to Love Homeless Housing in My Neighborhood." At the time, the shelter was nearly finished. "Pending a few more hurdles," he wrote, "we'll have a couple hundred new neighbors, and I'll be telling anyone who will listen what an honor it is to live across the street from A Bridge Home on Sunset Avenue in Venice. Without my daughter, I might not have come to the same conclusion."

About two years later, when we spoke, the housing center was up and running: 154 beds, hot meals and showers, case-management services. As a neighbor, Deuel said he experienced a gamut of emotions. On the negative side, there was fear for his family's safety, anger about drug dealers who operated flagrantly in the evenings, resentment for being made to suffer a project that would barely make an impact on an enormous scourge. At the same time, he knew that lives were being transformed. One shelter resident, a man named Gary, told him about person after person experiencing their lives being improved, with so much new-found self-respect. "One time Gary told me, 'At night there's nothing sweeter than the sound of a hundred clean people safely sleeping,'" Deuel recalled. "Gary's a pretty hardened dude, but he teared up saying that."

According to the website LAist, in 2020, as the coronavirus pandemic walloped the local economy, the city's Housing Authority began receiving more than a thousand applications per month for public housing, far exceeding recent averages. So, was it an honor, I asked Deuel, to live across the street from a bridge home, as he'd suggested in his article? Sure, he said, though it was probably too small a story to be heartwarming; more than sixty thousand people needed such services. "It's like putting a bucket under someone who's dying from a stab wound. It's so we don't mess our floors. But it's like with the buses. They have to park somewhere."

Deuel's daughter, now ten years old, still felt deep sadness seeing people on the street, and so did he, he said. What bothered him most was the violence—two nights before we spoke, a man was fatally stabbed on the Venice boardwalk—especially when so much of it was aimed at homeless people themselves. "I'm not some prissy homeowner who's upset with filth and chaos," Deuel said. "I kind of like filth and chaos. But the human degradation is so upsetting. I remember this one guy, going along on a BMX bike, and he was just slowly riding next to all these sleeping figures, screaming into their faces."

4.16 During the period this book was in the works, I installed an app on my phone to send me alerts anytime someone in our part of Hollywood wanted to announce an emergency. Most alarms were about missing pets. Next were suspicious men, men lurking in cars, men mad-dogging women, men shadowing people home from the grocery store. And then many went something like this: *TRANSIENT DO-ING DRUGS ON MY FRONT DOORSTEP. At 8:15 pm tonight I discovered a transient on my front steps shooting up heroin. He was disheveled and had needles spread out all over my stairs. I then immediately called the cops and it took them OVER AN HOUR to respond.*

The tone was typical, same for the air of normalization, suggesting that the affront wasn't so much the event as were the details. The heroin on the doorstep. The untidiness of the man, with his "spread out" needles. An offensive delay of the forces of law and order to make the problem go away. The messenger had felt a headwind. The future had arrived, and he or she needed to let us know, needed to make the narrative our narrative, to cry into the communal mind that they'd breached the gate, they were on our steps, *they* were doing this to *us* right now. The memo spoke of threat, but its theme was inevitability. People around L.A. often spoke of homelessness like it was preordained that one of the richest kingdoms in the wealthiest nation in human history would also lack the will to keep its citizenry safe—a hypothesis that felt like fact, even common sense, and consequently enabled people to talk about homeless people without ever talking *to* homeless people. Dan Johnson's idea about history was right. History in Los Angeles isn't chronological, but simultaneous. Our homeless citizens are not only our paradox but also representatives of time itself—demonstrating what had happened, what was happening, what was to come. They proved we were planning our obsolescence. We might have been grateful, if we'd noticed.

"In the confined urban spaces of the city-state, the instruments of sovereignty could easily be turned either to favor certain groups and families or to devastate them" (Lauro Martines, *Power and Imagination: City-States in Renaissance Italy*).

4.17 Suzette Shaw and I spoke twice during the coronavirus pandemic. Her voice was bright, her perspective long. Sheltering in her apartment, she had been reduced to local walks for exercise and was seeing more tents than ever, she said, also more white families on the street—probably due to the suffering economy? She wasn't sure.

She told me how, during the darker moments of her experience with homelessness, she'd been afraid sometimes to be alone with her thoughts, rehearing bad things people had said about her. Back then, going around Skid Row, there was a bridge in the neighborhood that she would walk across and think, *This would be a great place to jump from.* During lockdown, years later, she incorporated the bridge as part of her morning walks. "Now I can cross it," she said, "do a workout on that bridge, and my paradigm has shifted. It's a place I can go, regroup, and have wellness."

Shaw's trials were her testimony, her testimony her advocacy—and her advocacy was our chance to take action. Solving the homelessness problem was certainly within our power; what it required was people, from county officials to City Hall to ordinary folks, deciding to be less distanced, less narrow-minded. What she had meant, Shaw said, when she described poor people as being pathologized was that the rest of us tend to see them only in certain ways. Lazy. Wretched. Downcast. Criminal. "What people don't see is resolve—primarily, the resolve to sustain," Shaw said. "The resolve to keep alive a sense of hope."

False peaks • L-Age • Hollywood is a floating citadel • Imagining a world without nations • What we talk about when we talk about performance • "A dream times one million equals chaos" • Artists forged in collision • Validation karaoke • Interview with the Oracle of Los Angeles • The dream life of Henry Chinaski • "The horseman's mentality" • Religious visions • Diamond prospecting in California

5.0 To be recognized four times on the way to a 7-Eleven felt bizarre for the working actress. She didn't even look like herself. She had on winter gloves, dark sunglasses, black boots, a boxy coat color-blocked in red and blue. If anything, she looked like an art thief who'd just stolen a Mondrian from the Getty, but this was in mountainous Park City, Utah, during the Sundance Film Festival, where the actress was in town to promote a movie she'd dreamed up nine years earlier with a fellow waitress, and now her face was on posters, in programs, attached to party flyers. The night before, the film director Werner Herzog, one of her heroes, had wished her congratulations at a party. "It's crazy," she said, hustling down a crowded icy sidewalk. "It's crazy that it's even happening."

In mountaineering, a "false peak" is one that appears to be the top of a mountain until you reach it and see the real summit still looming, previously obscured from view. Hundreds of miles from the city-state, Park City sat among other peaks at seven thousand feet. Visitors sometimes experienced symptoms of altitude sickness; stores in town sold bottled oxygen. The actress paused to catch her breath, standing across from the theater where her film would premiere the following night. She didn't know if people would like it. "I hope they will," she said. "Obviously." Still, for a working Hollywood actress, wasn't getting into Sundance already the peak? If the movie turned out to be her break-through, with more peaks to come, what would that even look like? She was resuming her trek when it happened again: a woman crossed the street, turned around, and rushed over; she said she'd seen her on a panel that morning and she couldn't wait to see the movie. "I wish you so, so much luck," the woman said, squeezing both her hands.

Days were strange. Everything the working actress had done for more than two decades had been to reach this moment. It was everything she'd ever wanted. She had no idea if it would make any difference at all.

5.1 If you were assigned the role of Jen Tullock, you would be told that your height was five-four, your eyes penetratingly blue, your hair voluminous in an almost rectangular block of curls. You weren't Jewish, but you got that a lot. By birth you were southern, white, and gay, though from a distance the impression was less about variables and more the sum of your algebraic equation, $(hair + outfit)^2$. "It's my entire wardrobe," Tullock said demurely when asked about her many overalls and jumpsuits. "They're so forgiving."

Typical for many working actresses in the city-state, the talent was brimming, but the bank account was not. At the time, Tullock was renting a modest studio in a neighborhood adjacent to Hollywood. She did breathing exercises at night to reduce her financial angst. She was an atypical woman in her thirties, wearing her age in a fashion, by no conscious effort, that implied both millennial insecure-cocky and Gen X wizened-shrewd. When asked what she feared most in life, she said poverty, then drowning, then she thought about it more. "I'm scared of dying," she said quietly, "without having forgiven the people who hurt me the most."

"I really thought, I just thought, She has it," Mandy Patinkin said, recalling his first impression. Judith Light called Tullock one of the funniest people she knows: "There's a fullness of humanity, just joy and humor." During the year I shadowed her, people compared Tullock to a new Lily Tomlin, a young Bette Midler, a shorter Cher, suggesting a woman (with good hair) both present and period, contemporary and classic, someone who embodied a moment in style, humor, and politics, though in Tullock's case, for the time being, from a spot on the moment's circumference. And that was the trouble. As an actor, what was the point in being good if you went unseen?

In 2007, before Sundance, before Los Angeles, Tullock had moved to New York City with eighty bucks, a place to crash, and no job. Originally from Kentucky, she had attended theater school in the Midwest. In comparison, New York was gigantic and deafening. As a kid, she'd watched old movies about Manhattan, where every woman was gorgeous, every man spoke like he was on speed. "New York tells you it's romantic," Tullock said. "New York beats you over the head with its romanticism. It's like, 'Listen to this jazz you stupid fuck.'"

In New York she became a New York City Actress. A New York City Actress was intrepid. A New York City Actress was a hoofer. Each morning, the New York City Actress packed her bag with three costume changes, hit the streets, and pounded on doors. She wrote plays, did improv, performed one-woman shows. Attained milestones gradually, but always wanting more. "People love to post that bullshit inspiration meme on social media, 'Remember when you wanted what you currently have,'" Tullock said. "And I'm like, yeah, I agree with that sentiment, but also that forces you, in essence, to go into the past. And I have no interest in that." Mostly life was waitressing, auditioning, doing comedy in seedy basement clubs. "At the same time, I was bemoaning the fact that I was broke and not famous, and didn't like my body, and pretty girls didn't like me. But I was having the time of my life."

A year later she met another actress-writer-waitress, Hannah Utt. One day Tullock told Utt she had an idea for a movie: a pair of sisters find out that their mother, long dead, was actually alive and starring on a soap opera. Within a year they had finished the screenplay. Originally from Southern California, Utt moved back, and Tullock would fly out to visit, hunker down, and revise. Both were broke, subsisting on sweet potatoes. "It was pretty depressing, but then you'd get a ten-dollar residual check in the mail and go split a cocktail somewhere," Utt recalled.

Among a New York City Actress's biggest hurdles, or any actor's hurdles, was making a name for herself—and few gigs elevated a career like appearing on the big screen. In show business, California remained the compass point for manifesting destiny, with L.A. as the terminus. After nearly a decade in New York City, it was time to go.

5.2 Los Angeles probably has no single unifying dream besides the straightforward desire to be loved or not die in an earthquake—or perhaps not feel so alone in the vastness of the immense slouching shapelessness—but if there is one narrative that outsiders pin to the city-state, stocked with clichés but also some essential truths, it is often the dream of Hollywood.

No matter what industry a citizen works in, the entertainment business often feels like an alien ship hovering over the county, spewing out chemtrails that breeze around the world. Film, television, music. Icons of celebrity culture and "reality programming," including the Hollywood sign itself, erected in 1923 as a stunt to promote a real estate development. It was viewable from our block. Every day I watched tourists pose outside our house for a picture with the big abstraction—that embodiment of fame, stepping into the limelight, becoming "like the Hollywood sign itself, instantly recognizable," as Leo Braudy put it in *The Hollywood Sign*.

And yet the vast majority of Los Angeles has no more connection to "Hollywood"—the business, not the actual neighborhood—than the average moviegoer in Shanghai, except maybe the one time they saw a famous actor running errands. (A weekday morning, Ian Ziering, from *Beverly Hills 90210*, pushed a cart through the parking lot of a grocery store on Sunset and Fairfax, and a man lying on the sidewalk remarked loudly, "Looking big, Ian!" Ziering shouted back, "All natural! Protein, yo!") The actual neighborhood of Hollywood wasn't home to studios and stars, but instead many smack addicts, many two a.m. men looking to pay a little extra for a little extra, not to mention a long-standing Latin community, also elderly Russians. "We were still ethnic here," Karolina Waclawiak wrote in *How to Get into the Twin Palms*. "When people walked by, they would point at the windows and say things like, 'Why are they drying their clothes outside? Aren't they afraid they'll get stolen?'"

Of course, "Hollywood" was still very big business, big icon, big macher. And, in its own way, "Hollywood" *was* L.A. and the sign was L.A., and the people who worked in "Hollywood," the business that had for a long time mostly taken place in villages and neighborhoods scattered around the city-state that weren't named Hollywood—Toluca Lake, Burbank, Culver City—were also L.A., though those people often spoke as if everyone else in L.A. worked in the business of "Hollywood" too, which could be off-putting. As though everyone had friends in common from college in Middletown, New Haven, or Boston. Everyone had spent years afterward in Brooklyn or Austin. Everyone likewise communicated to one another in a way to suggest, whether or not they liked the work itself, that they didn't live in earthbound Los Angeles so much as in Hollywood's hovering citadel, a flying vehicle that occasionally drifted away to Atlanta, or Vancouver—or Park City, Utah—affording first-class views and snacks to those with union cards. As Carey McWilliams once wrote, "Where motion pictures are made, there is Hollywood."

So Hollywood was and wasn't "Hollywood," and Los Angeles was and wasn't "Hollywood," and these things got confused. But no matter the time of year, the spirit of "Hollywood" often seemed to say a lot about why people chose to live in the city-state in the first place, even if "Hollywood" did nothing for them at all.

5.3   Picture the modern world without countries: impossible. And yet nation states are only a recent invention. "Until the mid-nineteenth century most of the world was a messy sprawl of empires, unclaimed land, city states and principalities, which travelers crossed without checks or passports," Jamie Bartlett, author of *Radicals Chasing Utopia* (2017), wrote. "As industrialization made societies more complex, large centralized bureaucracies grew up to manage them."

Now try to picture the modern world without Hollywood. No stars, no films, no common global culture. No Mickey Mouse, no Barbie Doll, no Michael Jackson, no Kardashians. Also impossible, but maybe not so bad? Though perhaps no sense of shared dreams? "Everybody's living in the same movie. It's what we want to think" (Chris Kraus, *Video Green*).

5.4 In Hollywood, Jen Tullock was told repeatedly there were things she should and should not do if she wanted to make it. Don't be a contrarian. Don't be a tough sell. Don't wear your hair natural, it only makes you look dated. Try doing stand-up. Try doing stuff that's more marketable, more mainstream, or else people in the Midwest won't like it. The advice always came in friendly tones, but on a breeze of fatalism, like the advice women receive to survive in a world of men. Don't walk alone. Don't draw attention. Carry your keys in your hand like a fistful of knives.

In 2015, shortly after Jen Tullock arrived in the citystate, in her very first audition, she booked a "series regular," a main role, for a new HBO series. "I kind of showed up and was like, 'Well, I guess it's just acey out here, I guess New York was not meant to be for me,'" she said. The show was soon canceled. She auditioned for other big parts; producers looked elsewhere. She landed spots on shows, but they were one-offs. She got a writing gig, but it was temporary. Her first apartment was in an old hotel in Hollywood.

At that point, the HBO show was still locked. "I bought grown-up furniture for the first time," she recalled. "I was so proud of that place." When the show fell through, she tried renting out the apartment for extra income. Then her bank telephoned, wanting to know why she was writing so many checks to cash. A renter, she explained, had found her checkbook, drained her account, and wrecked the apartment in a multiday sex-drug rampage that left her new furniture destroyed.

Tullock's was a spangled keenness, but sometimes things got depressing. Like when a girl at a house party described a part she felt should have gone to Tullock, that she would have been perfect for—when maybe, unbeknownst to the girl, she had auditioned for the same role and been called back, then not given it for reasons beyond her control, a role that put another working actress on a red carpet in an expensive gown that was just one late-night internet search away. Advice echoed in her ears: Don't be an island. Get out more, go network. Why not work your way into a clique, like the Upright Citizens Brigade or another troupe? Think about being a little more like *her*, or *her*, or *her*.

5.5 In the original version of *A Star Is Born*, nearly every scene reinforces the movie's function as an advertisement for Hollywood. Released in 1937, it was the story of a young woman named Esther Blodgett, played by Janet Gaynor, who wants to leave North Dakota for Southern California. (It's a different picture from its many remakes, though one that likewise piggybacked off another great, *What Price Hollywood?* from 1932.) At the beginning, Blodgett's flinty Aunt Mattie is unfeeling about her niece's ideas. "She's just a silly little girl whose head has been turned by the movies. As soon as she forgets the whole thing, the better off she'll be." Blodgett responded, "Why will I be better off? What's wrong with wanting to get out and make something of myself?"

Between 1890 and 1930, the population of Los Angeles grew from fifty thousand to 1.2 million. The movie business transitioned at the same time, from silent films to talkies, low-class "flickers" to "the silver screen." By the 1940s there were more movie theaters in the United States than banks. The Hollywood Chamber of Commerce actually took out notices discouraging people from moving to Los Angeles. One ad I found showed a crowd outside an employment agency. "Don't try to break into the movies in Hollywood until you have obtained full, frank and dependable information," it said. "It may save disappointments." At the bottom it read "Out of 100,000 Persons Who Started at the Bottom of the Screen's Ladder of Fame ONLY FIVE REACHED THE TOP."

When Tullock arrived in Los Angeles, the town was experiencing a boom in hyphenation. In New York, as an actress who wrote her own material, Tullock had been encouraged not to hyphenate; to call herself an actor-writer suggested that she wasn't a good enough actor. Whereas out west, no one cared. Thanks to cheap digital equipment, actors were suddenly actor-directors, actor-editors. Anyone with a smartphone could make a movie and post it online. "The first question I hear actors ask each other now is, 'Well, what are you writing?'" Tullock said.

"A dream times one million equals chaos" is a quote attributed to Charles-Édouard Jeanneret, aka Le Corbusier, the modernist French architect. Based on conversations I had with about a dozen-plus Hollywood people—actors, managers, producers, agents, and directors, all of whom requested anonymity—it seemed that the everyday hustle of the film and TV business had changed dramatically, but in some ways not. First off, the cliché of a waitress on Sunset biding time to be discovered was dead. Thanks to the internet, the hyphenation era also applied to the ways actors supported themselves financially. They were driving rideshares, delivering meals, assembling people's furniture by the hour. They had side gigs as well, whether as voice-over artists or fit models or birthday clowns, and ideally, they also booked commercials each month. But the basic idea remained the same as for any waitresses of yore: maintain a flexible schedule in case an audition called.

One big change was diversification: casting directors finally wanted color. "Big shows like *Friends, Sex and the City*—you'll never see a show cast that way again," a talent manager said, meaning vanilla white. Not that people of color suddenly had it easy. The latest L.A. boom, known as "Peak TV"—in 2018, nearly five hundred shows, or "scripted originals," were produced; in 2010 there had been about two hundred—might have increased the number of roles for actors, but that was like building another lane on the freeway; it just filled up with more cars. (As of spring 2019, some eighty-one thousand people belonged to the Los Angeles branch of the Screen Actors Guild, and roughly seventy-four thousand of them identified as actor-performers, the Guild confirmed.) And Hollywood's love of stereotypes hadn't budged. The Funny Fat Friend. The Wife Who Likes Sauvignon Blanc. Of the half-dozen actors I interviewed, each knew their type with pinpoint accuracy, and they knew that to stray too far could mean less work, should agents deem them difficult. One man was Younger Brother Who's Good with Computers. A trained Shakespearean said his agent only sent him out for Prison Guard/Thug, because he was mixed-race with wide shoulders. Tullock said she was most often asked to read for Sardonic Best Friend. Basically, it came down to intangibles, the actors said. Maybe you paired well with another person in terms of chemistry. Maybe you and your scene partner had the right difference in height to match nicely (vertically) on a screen. Desired skin tone, desired weight, desired moxie—or conceivably you had none of those things. "For geeks, you really want to get someone who looks like they know what they're talking about," one producer said.

Another change: auditions now began at home. Actors were expected to submit recorded or "taped" performances first, rather than visit a casting agency—and there were upsides to it, the actors said. No getting stuck on the freeway. If you screwed up a take, you could film twenty more. At the same time, it was disheartening, always asking everyone you knew to spend hours "taping" with you, not to mention learning how to light, mic, edit, upload, and password-protect. One actor built his own taping facility to earn cash filming other actors. One actress outfitted her bedroom closet with professional lights. The biggest downside, several confessed, was the silence afterward, the lack of response when you didn't book the job. Basically, you were being ghosted all the time, and you were expected to weather it, ideally not care much about your career at all. "It's always the people that give zero fucks that are the ones that people want to cast anyway," one manager told me.

As a New York actress, Jen Tullock had been comfortable in the five boroughs, frenetic as the city. Los Angeles and its palm trees demanded different pacing. Traffic lights forced you to slow down. Traveling short distances took forever. "I think I used to think about my career on a linear timeline," Tullock told me. "It was like, once you've met these markers, then you can put the wax on the paper that says, 'You've made it.' And I will never feel that way. And that's something that also took me a long time to realize."

"It takes heroic effort to prioritize anything over proximity here, so you have to try very hard to make people like you. To be a person who is worth the trip, and to find people who are worth the trip" (Merritt Tierce).

At some point every day, often late, after another day of auditions, tapings, conference calls going nowhere, Tullock sat alone in her studio apartment and dreamed up a character. It was a meditation. Go to the little closet across from her bed, pick out an outfit, get dressed. Film a monologue on her phone, annotate it, post it online. "Disillusioned Witch Melts Down While Reading Shopping List to Assistant." "Perturbed Aussie Has Some Issues with Previously Misunderstood Stipulations of Her Trust Fund." A flip-book of roles no one had cast her in yet, and none of them "Sardonic Best Friend."

5.6 Since she was eight years old, the working actress told me she had dreamed of being in one of those Sundance photos in the gossip magazines: a smiling cast of performers standing in the snow, wearing puffy coats and winter hats. And then, against all the odds, after nearly a decade, what had been an idea between two waitresses seemed to be turning into something real. Tullock and Utt's script, *Before You Know It*, got the attention of a producer. Finances were scrounged, locations scouted. Utt would direct and co-star with Tullock. Alec Baldwin would play Tullock's boyfriend, Mandy Patinkin her dad, Judith Light the wayward mom. At a party that took place the night before they left to film, I watched Tullock swing between conversations, full wattage, actress on the rise. Near the bar, a young woman wore a T-shirt with Tullock's face on it. I'd never seen one before. She said she'd found it online. "I'm such a huge fan."

About a month later, during a video chat, Tullock looked wrung out. She'd been filming outdoors all day. Brooklyn was hot and muggy. "You forget how sweaty the summers are here." She added, laughing, "It's heaven."

Tullock once told me she had two reoccurring dreams, one about Jesus Christ, the other about her mother, and neither was good. It was complicated. At various times, hearing stories about Tullock's experiences from childhood, sometimes it sounded like a cautionary tale that had happened to someone else; other times it was still too close. Growing up, the family shifted between different homes around Louisville, Kentucky. Tullock's father had been a police officer, then a security guard. Her mother was a Christian recording artist. Tullock recalled a volatile relationship with her mom—unpredictable, harrowing. She didn't want to say too much. "Other people with an emotionally unstable parent say it's like sleeping in a war zone," she said. "You sleep with one eye open."

Mostly, growing up was about Jesus—the family attended an evangelical megachurch—but Hollywood got its due. Tullock's brother, Ryan, a professional musician, told me how, over and over, they watched MGM musicals when they were little. He remembered *Singin' in the Rain* playing at least once every two weeks for ten years. Some nights, Jen recalled, when things with their mother were particularly bad, she would cry herself to sleep listening to musical soundtracks on her cassette player. She loved Sondheim, specifically Mandy Patinkin in the title role of *Sunday in the Park with George*. Later, after Patinkin took the role as her father in *Before You Know It*, she told him he'd likely had a hand in preventing her from committing suicide.

At one point her brother asked me, "Did she say anything about Desmond?" When they were kids, he remembered his sister constantly inventing characters. "Desmond Montgomery" was a role she'd slip into to shield them; if Jen could make her mother laugh, the moment changed. Desmond became a family favorite, and started to receive presents under the Christmas tree, gifts meant for a middle-aged man—Nat King Cole records, cologne from a flea market. Tullock, thirteen years old, would thank her mom in character. "The tricky thing is that I kind of am a forty-five-year-old man," she said, laughing.

As a self-made person now in her thirties, Tullock knew that people like her often needed to put their pasts behind them, and sometimes could not. "It's informed a lifetime of anxiety and shame," she said one afternoon in a coffee shop. "But I have gained a sense of agency and pride in myself in only having done things in the way I believe in. That may sound moralistic or inflated, but I've stuck to my guns." It wasn't until I heard her say this, after months of interviews, that I realized she was someone forged in collision. And it was the collision of things—what she'd been steeped in over time versus what she had realized for herself; what she felt a person like her deserved and what such a person did not—that had produced some of her best performances and her worst impulses. The collision was at the center of everything.

Filming for *Before You Know It* finished in August. The deadline for submitting to Sundance was mid-September, and Sundance was the dream. For 2019, more than 14,000 movies would be submitted; *Before You Know It* was one of more than 4,000 feature-length films, and of those, only 112 were picked. "We were pretty fucking anxious," Utt said. "We were hopeful for the best but preparing ourselves for the worst." A few weeks after they submitted, Tullock and I met at a Mexican bar in a strip mall. She looked fried. For Sundance, all they could do was wait. In the meantime, she'd been up for a starring role in a Netflix show; it went to somebody else. She didn't get a part in a mockumentary series that had felt certain. Also, her car had been broken into, and she needed dental surgery, and she was considering driving down to Tijuana after her car was repaired to get the dental procedure at significantly lower cost.

She pulled out her phone to show me how she'd started making short films online for fans—a variation on her character studies—to raise money for her root canal. At first she charged $10 for a happy birthday message. Then fans offered a hundred dollars, a hundred and fifty dollars. She put down her phone. "I'm trying to live my life like I'll never get good news ever again," she said, grinning miserably.

Some weeks a check arrived, and the account was flush. Other weeks she wasn't far removed from the days of sweet potatoes. Everything was there, waiting to be called up, the talent, the passion, the desire. The silence from Sundance felt deafening.

5.7 The business of "Hollywood" had produced an odd vocabulary. An actor was "in" a movie but "on" a television show. In a screenplay, a character might be "aged up" or "aged down," or "colored up" if the character seemed too white. "Gaffers" were electricians, so were "best boys" and "best girls." "Apple boxes" were, well, apple boxes, which for some reason remained a staple of high-tech productions.

When a producer offered criticism of a performance or a script, they "noted it" or "gave notes," and for both actors and writers, receiving notes was a burden but also a sign of existence; getting notes meant you were working. One night, Rachel and I were invited to a dinner with a successful showrunner, a man who had created several big television programs. He told us his latest show's team of writers wanted to invent a doohickey you could hook up to a telephone, so anytime you had a "notes call" with executives, you could press a button whenever an executive made a comment and the phone would intone one of several prerecorded responses: *That's a great idea . . . I hadn't thought of that . . . You might be right . . . That's a great idea . . . You might be right . . .* The showrunner's phone rang. He left the table with an expression of worry. When he came back, Rachel asked, "So, when do the notes stop?" He looked somewhat shocked and explained that the call he'd just received had been from the head of the network, to give him notes on the scenes they'd shot that day.

How people in Hollywood see themselves, or are seen by others, often requires labeling. One afternoon, a successful film director at a party complained about "karaoke movie stars." A karaoke movie star, he explained, was an actor who wanted so badly to be a movie star that they came across as desperate; even if they became a star, they would always still only seem like one. Chris Pratt was the best example, he thought; in the sports world, Novak Djokovic? At a New Year's Eve party, an aspiring director, asked how the previous year had gone for him, said, "I was trying on the whole narcissism thing for a while. It was good, it was fine. But then I started losing my way. I just didn't have a sense of who I was anymore." One day at lunch, a writer friend said she'd been told that morning by a major movie star, during a conference call, that she was "the most fuckable thing in town." This was a few months before the Me Too movement began in earnest. In the same call, the star asked if she'd go on a date with a studio executive they knew in common, to potentially secure their project's financing. "You know how the town works," the star added. The friend didn't quite know how to answer; she told him she was busy, she was spending all day in bed writing. "Good, don't move, I'll send him right over," he said.

To be sure, the city-state had plenty of vocabulary that wasn't unique to Hollywood. A "sigalert" was a traffic snarl. "Gray May" referred to overcast weather, frequently extending to "June gloom." As exposed on the *Saturday Night Live* skit "The Californians," a habit remained to invoke highways with definite articles, as in "the 405" or "the 101," harking back to days when the freeways still had names, before they were assigned numbers. Like in the beginning pages of Joan Didion's *Play It as It Lays*, published in 1970, the protagonist Maria drives "the San Diego to the Harbor, the Harbor up to the Hollywood, the Hollywood to the Golden State, the Santa Monica, the Santa Ana, the Pasadena, the Ventura."

And the pink vans parked around Burbank advertising Topless Maids did, actually, represent housecleaners who worked seminude. There were also billboards on Sunset that advertised "Sugar Models," for anyone interested, either as sponsor or sponsee, in entering a transactional relationship. One near UCLA said, "Need a summer job? Date a SUGAR DADDY."

In Hollywood, when a producer summoned you to their office for "a general"—a get-to-know-you meeting—their assistant frequently would inform you ahead of time whether or not you would be "validated." The word applied mostly to parking. Producers' offices often had valet parking service, or were located in buildings with parking garages, and the phrase meant the producer would cover the garage or valet fee. But the broader meaning also had bearing. Producers perceived themselves as those who knew a good thing when they saw it. The best were curious and thoughtful. The worst ran on fear and envy. And some meetings with producers, being generally surreal, lacked labels. Rachel and I worked together as a screenwriting team. One morning we drove to Santa Monica for a kinda general, kinda not: a successful pair of producers wanted to turn one of our screenplays into a TV show. A friend of ours, acting as a go-between, met us in the lobby. The producers, two middle-aged white men, escorted us all into their conference room, and announced that they had bad news, they'd re-read our script that morning and changed their minds: they *weren't* interested in it, but since they booked the hour and we had parked in their garage, perhaps we would listen to some of their ideas? Ideas they didn't have yet but would fashion on the spot? Because maybe we'd hear an idea we found interesting, take it home and fashion it into a script "on spec"—a phrase producers use to mean "for free"—and bring it back to them to consider? Was that cool?

The men spun around in their chairs and faced a large whiteboard.

"How about this," the first said to the second. "Imagine a town from the nineteenth century that still exists today, undiscovered."

"Sure," the second said. "Is it in America?"

"It's in America," said the first. "Maybe in South America. No, America."

"Like, *The Land That Time Forgot*."

"Yeah, *The Town Time Forgot*."

"So, they have power? Electricity."

"Let's say they have power."

"But no phones."

"How's this, they're churning butter."

"It's like those Amish kids who get sent away for a year." The second producer turned to us. "You see what we're saying?"

"We want to see what these people are doing," the other one said. "The politics. Infighting and sex and stuff. What makes us tune in to the next episode? I need something to grab me, something to hold on to."

Silence for a moment while they turned back to the whiteboard.

"About that—" the first said in some confusion. "Do they know about the modern world? The people doing the butter churning."

"Maybe. But no phones."

"Maybe one or two people come in from the outside."

"Because there's a murder."

"No murder."

"But it's Shakespearean, it's gotta be Shakespearean."

"*King Lear*. Think motherfucking *Romeo and Juliet*. You gotta get some of that in there."

"They all want that," the second said to us dismissively,

and the first agreed, though it wasn't clear here who "they" were—the audience, the networks, other producers. "Look, this idea," he said, "maybe it's no good, but here's what you need to know: give us a world we've never seen before. That's what we want. That's what *they* want. Give us that."

After an hour more of this, the receptionist asked if we needed validation, we said yes, and she pasted several stickers onto a ticket stub to pay for our parking. Unfortunately, the parking attendant in the basement told us the receptionist had messed up: she'd only applied enough stickers for an hour's worth of parking, but the meeting had run an hour and fifteen minutes. A nonvalidated parking space in their garage cost $50 per thirty minutes. The meeting had cost us twenty-five bucks.

"Really the only thing you can hope for in a meeting like that is to not get fucked on parking," our friend said. "Like we just got fucked."

Hollywood is an interesting, strange place to work. In subsequent meetings, if things weren't going well, Rachel and I would look to each other and mime operating a butter churn. But sometimes it was easy to get flustered. One morning, we visited a big-wig producer at his offices in West Hollywood to pitch a film idea. In the conference room, six people sat around a modern coffee table. The table was dark and bare except for a small mirrored coaster and three lines of cocaine. It felt like a trap. Should we acknowledge the drugs were there? Did someone forget to clean up a party? Were the lines meant for us, akin to coffee? Later, Rachel figured out that it was something else: a coaster sold by the artist Nir Hod, printed with realistic-seeming white powder. "There is a certain magic in loneliness," the artist explained in his statement about the piece. "It's not about drugs or glamour—it's about the inside world, where you can dream and love and seek a greater truth—it's about a feeling of being connected to something so human."

The churn is real.

5.8 As an industry, Hollywood requires few raw materials besides flesh, and so, when tens of thousands of citizens in a densely packed region sacrifice their mental health and bone density to a business so unruly and determined by luck, where no one knows the lay and nearly every venture fails, it makes sense that the city-state is littered with mediums.

In the city-state, a citizen's sudden interest in mentalists, tarot cards, or hallucinogens would not be met with incredulity. Our nearest psychic was at the end of our block; the next was three blocks away. We knew of shamans flown in regularly from Peru to run hallucination ceremonies. In 2001, an investigation in the newspaper revealed psychics to be so integral to the Sinaloa Cartel's local operations that judges allowed the authorities to wiretap their conversations. One Compton psychic, the article said, would roll snail shells in order to warn her clients about informants—though, in 2007, after one was indicted on cocaine-distribution and money-laundering charges, she confessed, "These people give me money and I tell them what they want to hear. I don't know the future."

For a hundred bucks, two instructors in Topanga taught me how to communicate with vegetation. Afterward, I was "selected" for conversation by a sticky monkey-flower plant, and sat beside it for twenty minutes. I was supposed to hear its messages, but I did not.

Before a person met with the Oracle of Los Angeles, the Oracle asked them to face the street, eyes closed, while she cast spells, rang bells, and wove something smoking around their shoulders to cast off bad juju before entering her house. The Oracle, otherwise known as Amanda Yates Garcia, operated in Mid City. In her thirties, she was a medium, witch, healer, and something of a therapist and life coach to Hollywood types; I learned about her from two different television writers who had seen her for consultations.

In the back of the house, in a large room full of books and crystals, she would penetrate my unconsciousness four times, she explained, and experience visions. Both of us concentrated while she medium'd her way into me, or my space, or something, humming at a high pitch, her hands and body quivering. There were prayers to guides and undecipherable whispers. Then, for a quarter of an hour, she appeared to experience a series of deliriums, waking dreams that featured birds and bats, a crystal cave, and a bear who made her raise her voice. Finally, she returned, back "across the threshold," and we had a conversation for a while to see what had been stirred up, then a tarot reading that focused on a bad book review I'd gotten recently that I couldn't quite shake. Half an hour later, she suggested that on the next full moon I write out a petition, expunging the critic from my world, then burn the paper and cast the ashes into a graveyard, asking any nearby spirits for help in escorting the critic out of my life. Also, I should obtain a replica of my spirit animal, which she informed me was a bear, and build an altar around it. Finally, she thought maybe I should cut back on coffee, which I appeared to overconsume, judging by my twitching eyelid. (She was right.)

A year later, I saw Garcia profiled in the newspaper under the headline, "The working witches of Los Angeles just want you to be your best self."

5.9 Writing a book such as this, about the city-state and its humans and their wins and losses, eventually a person would be introduced to Henry Chinaski. What Chinaski had managed to do by his mid-forties—and only in the city-state of Los Angeles could he have achieved it, he believed—was to construct a life in which he made just enough money as an actor and lost just enough money as a gambler to be able to do exactly what he liked. And what he often liked to do, several days a week, was to go on a fourteen-hour marathon, ten a.m. until two in the morning, during which he'd run the bars in his little corner of the San Fernando Valley and play the ponies.

By noon on a bright autumn Thursday, Chinaski had been gambling and drinking for about ninety minutes in a dark bar in North Hollywood, the small valley town that was a fifteen-minute drive over the mountains from Hollywood proper. Chinaski had lived in the county for nearly two decades. In person, he had the broad-shouldered good looks of a former football player whom the universe had yet to strike with much grief. For fifteen years he'd been a horseman, he said when we shook hands, and had gained something he called "the horseman's mentality," which he promised to explain over the course of the day. "Horses are my Kryptonite," he said while ordering us a pair of beers. "I walk by a TV with a horse on it, I get the sweats."

A race was about to start. Chinaski picked up a newspaper and rolled it into a crop; his habit during races was to whack the bar like a jockey stoking his horse to a win. "So here's the two horse," Chinaski narrated quietly after the gun went off. "He's on the lead, that's where you want this horse to be, you see he's getting a little heat on the outside"—*whack* went the crop—"now we need this two horse to get out, watch the jockey to look under his right armpit, then we know he's got horse and he's going to blast out"—*whack whack* went the crop, and his voice picked up volume— "come on buddy just look, oh don't let this four go with you, come out on the four, whip him on the left hand side and come out on the four"—*whack whack whack*—"four's already all in! JESUS WE'RE HAND RIDING we might be loaded this four horse could be loaded oh man I need a wire"— *whack whack WHACK WHACK*—"and here comes the three on the inside two three get the exacta but do not let the three win OH SONOFAGUN don't do it to me stay up four GIVE ME TWO THREE FOUR AND ROSECRANS IS A FOUR-LEAF CLOVER"—*WHACK WHACK WHACK WHACK*—"TWO'S A WINNER, THREE'S COMING IN SECOND, TWO THREE FOUR SIX OH MY GOD WE DID IT WE HIT THE SUPERFECTA AND EVERY-THING!"

WHACK! WHACK! WHACK! WHACK! WHACK!

I had no idea what had happened, except the beers were empty, the crop was in tatters, and Chinaski was very glad to meet me, he said, while he ordered us another round.

"Los Angeles is perennially refreshing itself with new-comers who have left behind them the pressures for confor-mity" (Remi Nadeau, *Los Angeles: From Mission to Modern City*). The Chinaskis of Pittsburgh were a large, sturdy family of Catholic Czech Americans, Chinaski said, with roots somewhere outside of Prague. Chinaski, the youngest of six, much younger than the rest, had grown up babysitting his sisters' children. A gambler since he was thirteen, a life-long performer, he'd always dreamed big, but no one had encouraged his ambitions; no one thought he'd leave Pitts-burgh, but they hadn't made room for him either. "Anybody who's a little too loud, who doesn't want to give in, they reject you," he said. He moved to Los Angeles, and found a place that had room for him. A sense of being spurned still pissed him off. "[In Pittsburgh] you do anything out of the ordinary, you're viewed as weird. And if you get a little suc-cess, they root against you. And when you *are* successful, they suck your dick. I fucking hate that. I want everybody to win. Whatever you're into, I'm into it."

Gradually he found his way into acting: small parts in television and film, some national commercials. Around the bars and restaurants of the San Fernando Valley, specifi-cally North Hollywood, where Chinaski lived and mostly stayed, he was known well enough to be greeted cheerfully by the dozen or so bartenders and hostesses we encoun-tered. He knew their names, the names of the men on valet, the number of children in a line cook's family. "Oh, here we go," said one bartender loudly, an aspiring actress in her early twenties, who turned around as soon as she saw him and switched the television to the races. ("No one else ever watches [horses]," she said. "We love him, though.") For an hour Chinaski placed small bets, "cups of coffee," on several races, and lost all of them, but that was routine, he said. As a working gambler, the most he'd ever won on a single bet was $64,000. The most in a single weekend in Las Vegas: $100,000. The most on the Kentucky Derby:

$37,000. But mostly he lost, he said, smiling, then turned to the bartender and asked after her latest auditions.

All day and night, Chinaski was solicitous and generous, always picking up tabs, happy-go-unlucky with strangers and friends. It made me think that probably the only thing better than being Chinaski, in Chinaski's mind, would be to be a more winning Chinaski—a version ridden as fast and as far as a Chinaski's pumping heart could take him.

The biggest gamble of his life, he explained between races, was his acting career. He still had a dream to land something meaty, a regular role on a show, just some great lines in a great scene! In the meantime, he couldn't complain. "People are like, 'You could've contributed to the world,'" he said. "I couldn't! I'm limited. If I could be Elon Musk, I'd be Elon Musk. All I can do is be charming and open doors and get groceries for people, take people to the doctor. I'm good and nice, but not at a life-changing level; I just know my limits."

Suddenly a gun fired. Another race. He'd already placed his bets. He stood up and yanked out his crop. "Oh we got horse, we got horse, come on five, we got horse, come out on the six COME OUT ON THE SIX you're going to gun me down six, six got us done SHIT, SIX IS LIKE FALKOR FROM *THE NEVERENDING STORY!*" The race ended. Another loss. "Shit!" Chinaski yelled again, and sat down angrily on his stool. I asked how much he'd lost. He didn't answer, just drank his beer. "That was a big, big bomber," he said quietly to himself. A moment later, he said from the corner of his mouth, "What is the second-best thing to gambling and winning? Gambling and losing."

I asked if that was the horseman's mentality. He didn't answer.

A few minutes later, Chinaski checked his phone.

"Holy shit," he said quietly. He stood up. "Holy shit!"

"What is it?" the bartender said.

Chinaski looked at her, looked at his phone again, then stared out the door. His body went rigid. His eyes were suddenly glowing, as if the sun was in the center of his skull.

"I can't believe it," he whispered.

"What?"

"I booked a part."

"You did?"

"I booked a part!"

The bartender laughed. "There you go, Chinaski!"

He read out an email to the entire bar. It was from his television agent: he'd booked a gig the following week, a speaking role on a new police show. "It's two lines or whatever," he said, "but just get me on set, who knows what will happen?!"

"You're a charmer," the bartender reassured him. "You're charming!"

"If I crush one or two lines, then somebody might think, instead of casting Buffalo Bill or whatever, put in Chinaski—you gotta believe that!"

"Tough up or buck up, Chinaski," the bartender said, laughing, and put down two more beers.

5.10 "Chinaski," of course, is not his real name. Henry Chinaski was the literary alter ego used by Charles Bukowski, the Los Angeles writer who worked for the Postal Service for years to support his drinking, gambling, and writing habits—traits he loaned to his character Chinaski, in addition to a wistful, misanthropic self-awareness. "All a guy needed was a chance," Chinaski says in Bukowski's novel *Ham on Rye*. "Somebody was always controlling who got a chance and who didn't."

In this account, my Chinaski appears in disguise because, in a previous life, he had dabbled in the darker arts of the gambling world, though never enforcement, he said, nothing nasty. "You don't want a guy like me for that. You go to any county court or jail, find a UFC fighter that's on meth, say, 'Here's five thousand bucks. This guy owes me fifty. If you get the fifty, you keep the five. If you don't get it, you beat the shit out of him, you still keep the five.'" But Chinaski didn't like to talk about the past, he hated the past. We shuffled down the sidewalk, covering our eyes from the beating sun. Most of all, he wanted to talk about the energy of a gambler, he wanted me to understand the gambler's *why*. The gambler's energy was a magical energy, Chinaski believed, and it was the very essence of Los Angeles itself! "There's two forms of energy you want in life as a gambler," he said at our fifth bar. "You want people to be indifferent whether you win or lose; and you want other gamblers to lose. But one thing you do not want people to do, or you'll lose every time, is worry. If someone worries about you, you will never fucking win. *Worry* is a word that I wish was abolished. It does no good for me, it does no good for you." His face darkened. "The minute someone's like, 'Dude, I'm worried about you,' I fucking leave. I love when people hate on me, secretly rooting against me. There are people who want you to lose, there's people that are indifferent, and there's people that want you to win—I'll take all of those. The people who are like, 'Dude, I'm worried about you,' they're cancer for a gambler. That energy will bring down everything. I get a totem pole face when that shit happens."

"I know it sounds crazy but I came here believing—no, not really Believing—but hoping maybe, maybe somehow crazily hoping!—that some producer would see me, think I was Real—Discover me!—make me a Big Star!" (John Rechy, *City of Night*).

"Everywhere, ghosts. The longer he lives Downtown, the more years that pass—and now it is eight—the more he is haunted" (Dana Johnson, *In the Not Quite Dark*).

Initially, as Chinaski steered us from one bar to the next, North Hollywood lay flat and roasting, but gradually the night cooled things off. Throughout the day he'd lost around $1,000 on bets. There were drinking and food expenses that were likely sizable; not once, that I saw, did he allow anyone to pick up a check. In the afternoon, the gambling switched from horses to football. The party expanded to include fellow gamblers, hangers-on, men and women following us from bar to bar, accepting Chinaski's largesse, several of them deep in a bog of booze. Friends told me that Chinaski was mayor of the Valley. They described, yelling over the noise of televised sports, the women who camped out on his checkbook, whom Chinaski loved too much to evict. Going against Chinaski's rule of drinking only beer, around sunset there were shots and cigars to celebrate the TV part he landed, and sometime around beer twelve or thirteen, feasibly fifteen or sixteen, in a crowded bar where the owners liked Chinaski enough to allow him to smoke indoors, he came out of the men's room, found me, grabbed me by the shoulder, and said in my ear that he'd accidentally crapped his pants ten minutes earlier, so he'd gone to the restroom to clean up, only to realize that removing his underwear would be difficult if he didn't want to get his legs dirty—pulling down his briefs might cause a mess, but how were they to be removed otherwise? Then, inspiration had struck: Chinaski remembered the butane torch lighter in his pocket that he used for cigars, took it out and set fire to his waistband, quickly ripped it apart, tore off his undies, then blew out the flames and tossed the smoking shorts into the garbage can. He explained all of this into my ear before whispering, "You do not get exquisitely perfect days."

We parted in the neon dark around one a.m. at the entrance to an Italian restaurant. The only meal he ate was a late dinner, he said, to stay trim. A few minutes later I was waiting for a car, looking over my notes, when Chinaski came back, put his hand on my arm, and said, almost sadly, "'Risk a little, win a lot.' That's the horseman's mentality."

5.11 For a week each winter, while the brown hills turned green, the floating citadel of entertainment flew slightly east from the city-state, and a small mountain town became even more Hollywood than Hollywood itself.

To attend the Sundance Film Festival involved a sense of risk that even Chinaski might admire—Robert Redford once called it "Park City's version of Pamplona and the running of the bulls"—but more so an air of religion. Each January, much of the movie business, plus thousands of fans, established a tent city for a week in the midst of what felt like a pilgrimage. People embraced in the street. So much was described as "sacred" and "transcendent." Going by overheard conversations, everyone was having visions: moments of sublimity in amazing films, séances with augmented reality, the simple revelation of spotting Lupita Nyong'o stepping out of a Chevy Suburban. The holy days took place on the first weekend, when the cast of a film, plus a convoy of publicists and producers, marched through town like crusaders, sweeping in and out of rooms to pillage gift bags and repeat in interviews the same wide-eyed thoughts about their belief in one another, their faith in the journey, their commitment to Cinema and Art. No one seemed clearheaded. The air was thin, the alcohol gratis, the catering infused with CBD. The truly anointed wore festival passes on lanyards around their necks and tended to them like talismans, never to be removed. A man's frantic phone call on the sidewalk: "I think I lost my pass . . . I need a pass!"

One night, a festival volunteer, monitoring a queue of attendees who were hoping to get into a movie, said that she had previously visited Sundance like a normal person but could never obtain movie tickets; tickets during the first weekend were notoriously hard to snag. So now she flew in from Florida just to be a volunteer. It made sneaking into movies easier. "I love movies, what can I say," she said.

When Jen Tullock and Hannah Utt learned in November that their film had been accepted to Sundance, the reaction was an explosion of joy, then panic. For anyone with a film in contention, the festival felt like a gigantic audition, a referendum on whether or not you were any good. "What you made, either everybody likes it and you're a genius, or people don't and you're crazy," the actor Daniel Radcliffe said, sitting across from me during a media brunch. In the U.S. dramatic competition section, "the centerpiece of the festival," *Before You Know It* was one of only sixteen films accepted. Of those, 53 percent of the directors were women, 41 percent were people of color, 18 percent were LGBTQ+. The longtime home of Harvey Weinstein, Sundance now offered attendees a hotline for reporting sexual violence. Tullock guessed she'd had around a dozen #MeToo moments in her career. "Now male actors or directors say to me, 'Oh sorry, am I me-tooing you,'" she said. "They'll say it sarcastically, but they also say it as a safeguard. Because it gives them the opportunity to keep the moment open for a flirtation while also going on the record as having said, 'I know about this movement, and I know that I have to be held accountable.' Quote unquote, wink, wink."

If Sundance was nominally a film festival, opening weekend was unabashedly Hollywood's Spring Break. Crowds were rowdy, drunk and shouting, slipping on icy sidewalks. On Sunday night, at the top of Main Street, a convertible Bentley sat in traffic, top down, bass rattling, wrapped in technicolor chrome. At the premiere for *Before You Know It*, every seat was taken. After a brief introduction, the lights went down. The crowd was soon laughing—there were plenty of jokes—but mostly the movie was a story of abandonment. Tullock appeared in scene after scene, and her life-fullness, just hurrying through a room, became mesmerizing. Toward the end, her character had a moment with her mother, played by Judith Light, that left me in tears, and not just for the similarities to her own story; there was a fusion of awareness and spontaneity in the performance that seemed alchemical. I thought, to be a normal human going through a day is nothing special, but watching an actor do the same thing on-screen can be uncanny.

"There are some people who, without any contrivance, without any hint of showing off, walk across a room beautifully," David Thomson, the film historian and critic, told me later. "You couldn't do it. I couldn't do it. We'd be self-conscious. They understand that to walk across the room, four or five steps, can be a revelation of the soul."

The primary function of Hollywood had long seemed to be the making of stars: a person whose name we all knew, somebody we wanted to see over and over again. But why? Why do we want to see anything again that we've already encountered? What do they have that we want? For the same reason, I kept asking myself why I felt compelled to continue interviewing Tullock, to spend another hour gathering material I probably wouldn't use. Mandy Patinkin and I talked about it on the phone. "When you take someone like Jen Tullock," he said, "who is incapable of not being alive, she has an immediate addictive quality to anybody she comes in contact with. Because she is so alive. It's not just about being talented or brilliant or beautiful; it's about being hungry and alive for the few moments we're here. And some people have that. They care about the time they have on this planet a little more intensely than other people do. And everybody wants to drink from that cup."

The morning after the premiere, in winter coats and hats, the film's cast ran through a string of press events. It would be like this for a week: interviews, panels, additional screenings. In the afternoon they ate at a restaurant inside a tent reserved for industry folk. A crowd of dozens hovered outside the door, hoping to catch a glimpse. Demi Moore sat at a table near us. I asked Tullock if she ever got that Sundance photo, the one she wanted as a little girl. She grinned at me. "The first photo shoot we had, we were making small talk while the photographer was taking my portrait, and I just said, 'I gotta tell you, I have wanted to do this for twenty-five years.' He was like, 'Do what?' And I was like, 'This.' He was like, 'Cool. Face the light please?'"

5.12   After so much time spent with Tullock, in my attempt to understand the Hollywood hustle, it became difficult to remain writer-subject. Over a year and a half she came over frequently for dinner. She and Rachel became close. One Sunday morning Tullock escorted me to Mosaic, an evangelical megachurch on Hollywood Boulevard; I wanted to get a sense of how she'd grown up. After the service, the preacher baptized people in big plastic tanks on the sidewalk. Each person came out of the water shouting, "I'm all in!" This took place only a few blocks from Hollywood's Walk of Fame, where the sidewalk was embedded with stars. If only all breakthroughs were so easy.

At Sundance, *Before You Know It* played to sold-out crowds. Tullock was spotlighted by critics for stealing scenes. "A total breakout," one wrote. But the movie was not the talk of the town. It wasn't acquired for millions of dollars that week; it wasn't acquired at all. During the lunch in Park City, with Demi Moore sitting nearby, Tullock read something on her phone with a frowning look of concentration. An email from her mother, she said. Did it say what she wanted it to say? "It'll never say what I want it to say."

Like every human, the working actress was easily wounded. At her worst she was quick to lick blood from a scratch. At her normal, she was a complex, intelligent person in a business that wanted defined types. And at her best she was a great actress, probably something more. "She's been through so much and had to see the world from so many vantage points, she's able to empathize in a way that helps her connect," Utt said. "She doesn't need to process how she feels." After Sundance, we kept in touch, and Tullock kept busy: writing a new screenplay, workshopping a musical, constantly auditioning. She had the Hollywood mentality, the horseman's mentality, and if some of her nicer clothes needed to be sold to Goodwill to help pay the bills, so be it. And then, nearly twelve months after that, Tullock was cast in a new show, to be directed and produced by Ben Stiller, where she'd star alongside Patricia Arquette and Adam Scott, with paychecks big enough to erase her debts.

But before all that, only two months after Sundance, Tullock telephoned because she'd landed a brief part in an episode of a new sitcom. The episode was shot on a ranch on the city-state's outer fringe. At one point her phone rang, and she walked offset. A few moments later she was leaping up and down. *Before You Know It* had been acquired. It would play festivals through the spring, open in theaters over the summer, and then be viewable inside the monitors of seats on airplanes, among other places. She would be seen.

"There are several possible ways in which to prospect for diamonds in California. One way, and perhaps the one most likely to yield a specimen stone, is to search the places in which diamonds have already been found" (Mary Hill, *Hunting Diamonds in California*). Hollywood was a town of false peaks, but a small number of people still reached the top. Who's to say which summit was true? Jen Tullock was a working actress in Hollywood because, when she was six years old, she saw Barbra Streisand in *Funny Girl* and thought, *That's me, that's my future.* One afternoon, at a café in Beachwood Canyon, directly beneath the Hollywood sign, she was asked, what is the value in pretending to be someone else? "I'm at my best when I'm someone else," she said after a moment. "I get to tell the truth with no consequences. I can tell the darkest and most terrifying truths about human nature with zero consequences. The consequences exist within the parameters of the scene. And when they call 'cut,' I'm free."

LESSON 6

What Happens Next Door Happens in Madagascar

The marine, the fire, Malibu • Naming the beast • Welcome to the Pyrocene • The truly Californian • The Point Dume Bombers • When "the patrons and purveyors of culture shut their eyes" • An argument for burning • Creature comforts • Einstein doesn't know from earthquakes • Emergency management • Living in an "Earthquake-induced liquefaction area" • Mild hypothermia • Debris flow • "Time, time, time . . ."

6.0 Raised on the city-state's watery fringe, Robert Spangle had been unusual for a student at Malibu High School: right after graduating, he joined the U.S. Marines, deploying to Afghanistan in 2009 and 2010. Spangle was a radio telephone operator in Force Reconnaissance, one of the Marine Corps's special operations. They performed intelligence gathering thirty miles or more behind enemy lines, he explained, or one hundred nautical miles behind any national boundaries that were oceanic. Spangle was part of a team of six, running communications between soldiers on the ground or with aircraft flying overhead. "You have two or three massive radios you carry out, for long-haul communications," he said. "If set up correctly and you're in a good position, you can pretty much talk all the way around the world. But that's very finessed, with a lot of antenna work and a good position."

The first time we spoke on the phone, in November 2018, Spangle was calling from what might be characterized as a bad position: the middle of the worst fire his hometown had ever seen. Disobeying a mandatory evacuation order, Spangle had stationed himself on a bluff overlooking Malibu's coastline, operating as the eyes and ears for an ad hoc crew of young surfers who were driving around in pickup trucks, trying to put out fires, save houses, and rescue people stuck inside. "Outside of some combat scenarios, this has been the most insane week of my life," Spangle told me.

Days earlier, having returned from an overseas assignment—after the marines, he'd built himself a career as a photographer—Spangle almost died in a motorcycle wreck on the I-10. The bike wound up totaled. Spangle's foot, trapped under the bike, was nearly totaled. "The skin on the top of my foot was just pulverized," he said. A friend drove him to the cottage he was renting on Point Dume, where he drank three beers and fell asleep. The next morning he woke early, realized he needed to go to the hospital, then looked outside. "Normally it's a bit foggy here in the morning, but this was black and gray on the mountaintops. It didn't look right. I was like, 'No, that's fire.'"

That same morning, after a swim in Venice, I'd been staring north, looking up the beach at a gargantuan cloud, magnificent, a roiling head of gray and black smoke arriving like something out of a doomsday film. The news announcer on the radio said that a wildfire begun the previous day in Woolsey Canyon, near Simi Valley, had been fanned overnight by Santa Ana winds into something much, much worse.

Woolsey would prove to be the biggest fire in Malibu history, torching some ninety-seven thousand acres, the most destructive fire in Los Angeles and Ventura County history up to that point. Other stories competed for airtime, though, at least in the beginning. That week, the Camp Fire was burning in Paradise, north of Sacramento, and would become the state's deadliest. Locally, the Hill Fire was being fought about fifteen miles west. Then there was Borderline. Just one day earlier, twenty miles from Malibu, the inland community of Thousand Oaks had seen a former marine kill thirteen people, himself included, at the Borderline Bar and Grill, a country tavern popular with college students who liked to two-step. Nate Rott, a reporter for National Public Radio, covered both incidents, Borderline and Woolsey, crisscrossing the mountains. "With breaking news, there's usually a big shot of adrenaline that kicks in," Rott told me later. "The challenge is carrying that through the length of the event." A former wildland firefighter from Montana, Rott spent the week interviewing families, some with members involved in both disasters. It was a struggle to keep up, he said, physically and emotionally. "The back-to-back wrecked me. I was exhausted and burnt out for days."

Inside the fire, waking up with a damaged foot, Spangle knew that he needed to evacuate. He packed his car, alerted his neighbors. "Man, you talk about a Los Angeles crowd," he recalled, laughing. A woman in her sixties was a yoga instructor. The other neighbor was a young aspiring tech guru who didn't think much of car ownership and preferred to take rideshares. "I felt pretty conflicted, actually," Spangle said. "The military side of me is like, 'You're responsible for your element, and their well-being is 100 percent your responsibility.' In military situations there's no such thing as free will. You do what you're told, and everyone has to act for the betterment of the element, the community. So, I was aware, I'm a bit conflicted here. I can be very much a brainwashed marine. 'You, get in the car, you get the supplies, we're moving in fifteen minutes and we're not stopping for fucking anything.' But the other side of me was like, 'No, these are civilians, and if they want to die, they can die. They have free will, and I don't have the right to tell anybody anything.'"

Meanwhile, Malibu was clearing out, cellular service had gone down, the young guru was worried—how would he obtain a Lyft out of town?

Spangle said he joined the military, in part, from seeing his country attacked on September 11. As Malibu burned, similar feelings were evoked, and his training proved useful in multiple ways. To begin, he convinced his neighbors to follow him down to Zuma, a large beach known as a safe place for local farmers to bring livestock during fires. People rode horses on the beach. Banks of smoke cascaded down the mountains. It looked like Steve McCurry's photos of the first Gulf War, Spangle thought, with clouds the color of asbestos. The wind smelled of wood smoke, burning eucalyptus, wild sage. Families were arriving with hogs in their cars. Donkeys brayed from trailers. Llamas were tethered to lifeguard stands. "They cut open a storage shed on the beach to put animals inside, and I remember this horse went in and cut its neck and was just braying and bleeding everywhere," Spangle said. At the same time, the foothills were on fire, and embers flew across the Pacific Coast Highway like red wasps—a highway that people had thought was unbreachable. "You could see people's eyes totally dilated. Nonsensical. Fixated on tiny things. And panic. Seeing a lot of people panic."

Which meant, for their element, it was time to go. Spangle issued a convoy brief straight from Afghanistan: "We're going to go 60 mph regardless of the speed limit. We're going to stick to the inside lane. If you need me to stop, you honk twice, and you keep honking twice until we stop. If we lose each other, we go back to the last intersection. Our limit of advance is once we get to the Palisades. Once we're there, we're fine." Later that afternoon, at a bar in Santa Monica, twenty miles east, Spangle was impatient for word from Malibu. His unit had gotten out safe. In Santa Monica, no one had a clue. "This is one of the fractal, amazing things about Los Angeles," he said. "Literally what's going on a couple neighborhoods away is as relevant or irrelevant as what's happening on the East Coast." The bouncer at the bar even gave him a hard time for wearing what Spangle termed "techno ninja stuff," tactical clothes that would be good for fire, not to mention a cane he'd fashioned from a stick. "The guy didn't even know there was a fire. He's like, 'Are you Gandalf?' I was like, 'No, my fucking home's burning down.'"

6.1 "And I saw what looked like a sea of glass glowing with fire and, standing beside the sea, those who had been victorious over the beast and its image and over the number of its name" (Revelation 15:2).

6.2 The city-state did not suffer cyclones, blizzards, or great freezes, but it knew flooding, earthquakes, and fire.

For the most part, floods were a distant memory. After devastating overflows in 1914 and 1916, the Los Angeles River was paved, reducing its danger. And though earthquakes arguably created Los Angeles—its shape and setting, its sense of unease and possibility—a great earthquake hadn't struck since Northridge in 1994. Everyone still feared the "Big One," looming in the future, though, judging by people's nonchalance, out of sight, out of mind. Then there was fire. The county burned with such regularity, it felt constant, almost year-round, as reliable as a stoplight, as much a part of the local aesthetic as Dodger hats or strip malls.

Smoky air, a red sun, ash snowing on your car. Thanks to the climate crisis, the fires were likely going to get more frequent and wilder, not just in California but across the American West. Steve Pyne, author of *Fire: A Brief History*, suggested that the trend could deserve its own era in time. "So vast is the magnitude of these changes that we might rightly speak of a coming Fire Age equivalent in stature to the Ice Ages of the Pleistocene. Call it the Pyrocene."

"If it is true that trends move from west to east," Joel Garreau wrote in *The Nine Nations of North America* (1981), "then Los Angeles is at ground zero of the future."

For residents of the city-state, fire was a rolling arson machine. In 1953 the Monrovia Peak fire was said to have released as much energy as five atomic bombs. Fire was also commonplace: bonfires on the beach, protest fires in the street, sidewalk grills for carne asada. In 1965 Johnny Cash, singer of "Ring of Fire," accidentally burned more than five hundred acres in nearby Los Padres National Forest while he and his nephew were out fishing. (Later, asked if he'd started the fire, Cash blamed his truck—"and it's dead," he said, "so you can't question it.") Fire was not only seen as inevitable; it was seen everywhere. In several years of driving the county's freeways, I passed a small wildfire at least four times. Artistically, references brimmed over—the fire art of *Day of the Locust*; Francesca Gabbiani's fire paintings; "The city burning is Los Angeles's deepest image of itself" (Joan Didion). Fire was also exciting, no matter its deadliness. During big burns, private citizens often launched drones, presumably to get a closer look, which would immediately ground any nearby water-dropping helicopters for fear of a crash. It got to a point that, according to the newspaper, the state of

California launched a public service campaign in 2015 with a TV commercial titled "If You Fly, We Can't."

"Fire in the street / Burn, baby, burn / That's all I wanna see" (Kendrick Lamar, "The Blacker the Berry").

In the summer and fall months, known locally as fire season, friends across the area talked about waking up from dreams of burning. Even L.A.'s prisoners fought wildfires, in a localized use of the Thirteenth Amendment's allowance for slave labor—a dollar an hour plus two dollars a day. And surely a callous citizen somewhere had volunteered the homeless to fight them, too. Or maybe not: according to the newspaper, overtime costs for firefighters surged 65 percent in the last decade, with annual wages increased to nearly $5 billion. In fact, thanks to overtime pay, some L.A. firefighters were among the highest-compensated workers in local government. In a recent fiscal year, eighteen sworn employees of the Los Angeles Fire Department earned more than $200,000 in overtime. One made $360,010 in overtime alone.

Fire was also how the city-state honored its least known. Annually, since 1896, the county buried the cremated remains of its unclaimed dead in a hole dug for a mass pauper's grave in Boyle Heights' Evergreen Memorial Park and Crematory, for those citizens whose stories might not otherwise be noted.

6.3   Fire was also seen as endurable. In the city-state between 1990 and 2010, more than eighty-five thousand new houses were built in areas of high risk. It seemed part of a statewide inclination, property developers building wherever they liked while shoveling big money into political campaigns. In comments defending his refusal to block homebuilding in areas at high risk for wildfires, the governor said in April 2019, "There's something that is truly Californian about the wilderness and the wild and pioneering spirit." And so, every taxpaying Californian was asked, realizing it or not, to finance the protection of homes built in places where fire was sure to burn.

"I wonder a bit at the ethics of this: How much pleasure should I take at a destructive, beautiful force?" (Ander Monson, *I Will Take the Answer*).

6.4 The Woolsey Fire would blacken hills, savage trailer parks, leap the Ventura Freeway, and burn until it reached the water. As it roared, news reports focused on the number of civilians killed, a thousand-plus buildings destroyed, more than two hundred thousand people evacuated. In the last ninety years, the area had burned at least thirty times, but not like this. As a result, much of the city-state felt like it was on fire. On the Westside, the air in your lungs was pure smoke. In East L.A., women outside a Laundromat wore face masks. The sky, seen from Downtown, became a sooty gray dome, with the sun behind it brightly orange, like a shimmering yolk.

At the same time, talk in the media and among people was often matter-of-fact, even dull—natural disasters being some of the area's most domestic events. In *Los Angeles: Biography of a City* (1976), LaRee Caughey said of the 1933 Long Beach earthquake, "In that first shuddering instant, as I had moved toward the children, the floor surged up and took the soup pot from my hands. When we came back in, I was not surprised to see it sitting in the middle of the floor." "Mud slides, brush fires, coastal erosion, earthquakes, mass killings, et cetera. We can relax and enjoy these disasters because in our hearts we feel that California deserves what-ever it gets." (Don DeLillo, *White Noise*). The same pose applied to gun violence. The Saugus High shooting (2019), the Fresno party shooting (2019), the mass shooting and at-tempted bombing in San Bernardino (2015)—and still, when such events occurred only a few neighborhoods away, they felt like they were happening in a different city, on another coast, or on the other side of the world. (Los Angeles's an-tipode, its geographical opposite on the planet, was a spot off Madagascar.) "The hardest thing for me about covering natural disasters and shootings, particularly the latter, is this sense of helplessness and inevitability you hear from people," Nate Rott, the NPR reporter, told me. "'It was only a matter of time before it happened here'—I can't tell you how many times I've heard that at shootings. People have just sort of accepted mass shootings as an ugly, unsurprising part of our modern world. And that's really hard, as a human, to hear."

For Woolsey, the police locked down Malibu with evac-uation orders, but people stayed behind anyway. A day af-ter leaving, Spangle, the former marine, snuck back in, if only to feel purposeful. "I knew, at the very least, if I go up there, I'm not going to get anybody else in trouble," he explained. "And I have enough experience to know when I'm in over my head." Inside the fire, the air was thickly black. Visibility was less than a city block. It looked like midnight at noon, he recalled. Burned-out cars, burned-down houses. Spangle's little shack was still standing, but houses on the street were torched. At the same time, new fires flared in the dark and prowled the hills. From Point Dume, he spotted a blaze in a gully a couple of blocks away. He drove down, and talked to an older couple dozing in their SUV. They'd lost their home. They'd been awake for fifty-something hours. Their eyes were dead. "I'd seen this in other situations, where that fundamental humanity, that human bondage, isn't there. They were done."

Then help arrived: a pickup truck showed up full of young men in particle masks, with shovels and buckets. Spangle felt a little self-conscious about how he looked—a thirtysomething ninja with a broken foot and a wizard's cane—but asked if he could join them anyway. "I knew them as the younger brothers of guys I went to high school with. They were a big surfer crew." He added, "I know Malibu and I know surfers, and they're fiercely loyal. If you're not a surfer, they don't know you. But I didn't really care. I just knew I was excited to find some people who were organized and trying to do something."

Which is how Spangle came to enlist with the Point Dume Bombers, and proceeded to attempt to save the neighborhood. Rolling through the smoke, attacking fires, snapping shovel handles by the hour. The group was named in homage to an old Malibu surf team. Guys fell asleep standing up. Vans melted on their feet. Spangle's primary task was to serve as a spotter: atop Point Dume, he scanned for fires through binoculars, then would radio down locations to the trucks. At first, all they had for communication was a pair of Fisher-Price walkie-talkies. Spangle, calling on his experience as a marine, showed them how to rig up makeshift antennas. Abruptly, with decent positioning, they could talk for distances up to a mile.

Within a few days the group was more organized. High-quality radios, multiple strike teams, makeshift headquarters. On Point Dume, Spangle equipped himself with a hand-drawn map, a camp table, and a sleeping bag. By day, he kept watch and the crew put out fires. The same thing at night, except he'd get into a cycle where he slept for forty-five minutes, watched fires for fifteen minutes, then tried to sleep again. The hours blurred together. Fires snaked through the streets. Spangle remembered one fire being especially difficult, a beachfront property that suddenly erupted one night in a wall of flame. It took them two hours to figure out how to find it. Finally, when they reached it, they discovered a surprise: the house had been decorated with solar-powered lights meant to imitate tiki torches, lights that, from far away, in the midst of a wildfire, looked convincingly real.

By the fifth day of Woolsey, all kinds of impromptu relief efforts were underway by multiple groups of volunteers: rescuing animals, helping people stuck in the canyons, cooking vast amounts of food despite the absence of electricity. At that point Spangle and crew were dealing less with dousing fires, more with delivering provisions to people who'd stayed behind. Supplies reached them by small boats off Paradise Cove. The Bombers would paddle out with surfboards and kayaks, then swim the goods back to shore—boxes of food, gallons of gasoline. Spangle was more worried than ever. "It's pretty intuitive what to do when there's a fire. You have a shovel, you have a fire," he said. "But relief efforts are different. You have pretty delicate emotions there with people who are exhausted and afraid. That's not something young men are predisposed to be good at." In the military, Spangle had conducted multiple amphibious operations. Without a pier, a situation involving small craft offered multiple risk factors: open propeller blades, people swimming nearby. Plus, in Malibu, pretty much everybody was an amateur, not to mention exhausted. Among the more treacherous moments were the times when the firefighting airplanes, capable of scooping up great bellyfuls of ocean, needed to refuel. In the military, Spangle had helped guide in attack aircraft. From Point Dume he noticed that the airplanes' path, when reloading water, was directly in line with the supply boats coming in—and neither group was communicating with the other. "I was like, that's potentially a bigger fucking disaster than the fire right now." Essentially, Spangle became an air traffic controller. The planes were on a seven-minute circuit. When they took off, he'd move the bezel on his watch and time it. Thirty seconds into the seven minutes, he'd send in the boat at full speed or tell them to back off if they were moving too slow. "For me, this was fucking terrifying," he said.

That week, outside of the evacuation zone, no one knew much. By the time Spangle and I finished our first phone call, my body was covered in ink; we'd been trying to connect for days, and when we finally spoke, I was walking down the street on the other side of town without a notebook, so I sat on the sidewalk and transcribed our conversation on my legs and left arm. But I was grateful for every detail. Frequently, the news that week focused only on the trials of the Westside's wealthy, like how Kim and Kanye had hired private firefighters to protect their $50 million estate in Calabasas; Martin Sheen, thought to be missing, turned up at Zuma in a visor and Hawaiian shirt. Carey Hart, a celebrity motorcycle racer, posted a picture online of a dozen men wearing sunglasses, masks, and bandannas, holding rifles at some kind of checkpoint, with a piece of wood spray-painted LOOTERS WILL BE SHOT ON SITE! Hart noted in a caption: "It's unfortunate that some people take advantage of others in a crisis. While the malibu fires have been burning, some locals have been fighting off and defending their property against the fires. There have been sightings of looters breaking in to homes. Well, if you are a looter, think twice if you are heading back into malibu. #DefendYourLand #2ndamendment."

According to Rebecca Solnit's *A Paradise Built in Hell*, this sort of fear-driven apprehensiveness was termed "elite panic." Thomas Coyne, a local survival expert who trained military and police units, explained to me that several things about the photograph were worth noting. The street behind the men appeared to be untouched by fire. The men seemed unfamiliar with firearms beyond what's seen on movie posters—several were pointing them at each other's heads. Regarding the variety of weapons, Coyne imagined the likely scenario was that one of the guys owned half a dozen long guns and had passed them out to his friends; then someone instructed them to pose for a photo, so they could aspire to pass in the virtual realm as turf defenders, true patriots, while in reality they were likely worthless, even dangerous.

6.5 "The patrons and purveyors of culture shut their eyes and dreamed of their farms beyond the city walls or the surrounding waters" (Lauro Martines, *Power and Imagination: City-States in Renaissance Italy*).

6.6 During Woolsey, many people on social media quoted Octavia Butler, as though she had foretold the Pyrocene. "One of my friends tweeted back, *Octavia knew, Octavia knew*," the author Lynell George told me. The same held true for work by Mike Davis. In "The Case for Letting Malibu Burn," a chapter from *Ecology of Fear*, Davis argued that taxpayers shouldn't keep forking out to rebuild a wealthy district that predictably burned to the ground every couple of decades. Davis and I spoke on the phone a few days after Woolsey started. What did he expect to see once the fire was extinguished? "Bigger mansions," he said flatly. One of his former students, he explained, was heir to a great California fortune, and the man had told him that right after the 1993 fire that burned Topanga Canyon, he and his wife had driven around looking for real estate to buy. "On the flip side, it always creates lots of jobs," Davis said. "Think how many construction workers it puts back to work."

During the pandemic in 2020, two months into lockdown, Davis aired similar concerns in an interview with the Los Angeles journalist Jeff Weiss. "Mom-and-pop landlords are weeks from liquidation, and the real estate investment trusts are looking over their shoulder, licking their chops, ready to buy property, knowing prices will never be this low again. It's an extinction event for your little neighborhood bistro but a huge business opportunity for the wealthy to come in and clean up."

Nearly a year after Woolsey, I met Spangle in Malibu for breakfast. Some hills were still charred, some were green. New mansions were under construction, filigreed in McMansion style. Just as Davis had predicted, I didn't see any new housing that might be deemed affordable. Bearded, watchful, Spangle arrived with a camera around his neck. After his military service, he had done war reporting in Kurdistan and northern Iraq. "[Woolsey] was the first time in my career I made the decision, and I was aware I *had* to make the decision, to not be a photographer," he said. "Either I'm a first responder or I'm a journalist. There's ethics behind that, but I had to decide on one role if I was going to do it well at all. Which was hard. I've been in emergency situations where I'm a photographer and feeling torn to be involved."

I asked what stood out in his memory aesthetically when he looked back on the fire. "Visually it was terrible and terrifying. Very, very powerful," he said quietly. "A lot of surreal moments. How unfamiliar the familiar can become. People couldn't recognize their own houses. I took a photo one morning, and it looked like a black-and-white photo. There just wasn't any color there. Visually it was quite stunning, but as a local, this is your backyard and you no longer recognize it."

For Spangle and the Point Dume crew, an upshot from the fire, once everything was contained, had been an intense sense of community. The group started a charity. They still got together regularly. For some, Spangle said, the force of their bond had been so powerful, they suffered depression after, something he'd guarded against himself, based on similar experiences in the marines. "I expected it to be like the end of a deployment. The closeness these kinds of disasters bring is a really rich experience. It's very fulfilling to be around people you not only trust but can really bare your soul to. The joy of everyone working together with the same goal in mind, sacrificing to that same goal—that's not something we have in our society anymore. We're very individualistic. It's an American thing, it's a modern thing." Was it a Los Angeles thing? Spangle nodded. "For a lot of these guys, it was the first time they'd ever had a touch of that."

In *War Is a Force That Gives Us Meaning*, Chris Hedges wrote, "The enduring attraction of war is this: even with its destruction and carnage it can give us what we long for in

life. It can give us purpose, meaning, a reason for living."
Spangle recalled how, on the fifth day of the fire, the crew
realized they needed a break. Also, the surf was up. They
silenced their radios, went down to the beach. Everyone
was covered in dirt and sweat. No one had slept much in
five days, let alone bathed. By that point, the fire was pretty
much controlled. There was a little bit of smoke but not a
lot. The beach they went to was below massive cliffs. Everyone took off their clothes, put on wet suits, paddled out
in water that was clear and emerald green, as if nothing
had happened. "One of these kids said, 'I'm glad water's
still the great equalizer,'" Spangle said. "And that was beautiful, this untouched element that makes Malibu what it is:
the surf."

That night, the group listened to music over a car ste-
reo and drank warm beer. Someone figured out how to hook
up a portable generator to a tattoo gun, and they gave each
other keepsakes. "Just like fire, a sense of community can be
exponential," Spangle told me. "A few guys in the beginning
decided they would stay and fight and figure it out. Other
people like myself saw that and decided to join in. This became something that preserved the greater neighborhood
and became a change of spirit. It's an old way of doing things.
You stay, you fight, you dig in. That's the Malibu way."

6.7 "Therefore comfort each other and edify one another, just
as you also are doing" (Thessalonians 5:11).

6.8 Feared most in the city-state wasn't fire, however, but fore-
shocks, quake, the Big One, an earthquake that scientists

expected to break sometime soon along the San Andreas Fault and ravage the land. A 2008 report, "The ShakeOut Scenario," issued by the U.S. Geological Survey, noted that, on average, the southern San Andreas Fault had generated earthquakes of a 7.8-magnitude or worse every 150 years. The last in Southern California, the 7.9 Fort Tejon quake, had occurred in 1857.

"Plate motions are benign, fatal, eternal, causal, beneficial, ruinous, continual, and inevitable. It's all in the luck of the cards" (John McPhee, "Disassembling California"). One week in 2019, while this book was being written in a borrowed house with a swimming pool, the Ridgecrest earthquakes rolled through, magnitudes 6.4, 5.4, and 7.1. A minute beforehand, I would swear the air had a strange crackling hush. It smelled different, like smoke from an electrical fire. Still, I didn't fully understand what was happening until midway through, when the lights in the kitchen swung drunkenly, the swimming pool spilled out of its basin, and the whole house felt like a rocking boat.

People *not* noticing earthquakes occur wasn't so unusual. The Dodgers, during a home game against the San Diego Padres in 2019, played through a 7.1 magnitude quake without noticing it on the field. In a 1980 interview with Hertha Gutenberg, wife of seismologist Beno Gutenberg, the director of Caltech's Seismological Laboratory from 1946 to 1957, I found a story about Albert Einstein where Gutenberg described her husband and Einstein walking across campus, deep in conversation, not discerning an earthquake taking place under their feet until a colleague pointed it out. "[Physicist] Richard Tolman told them, 'Now you have your earthquake,'" Gutenberg said. "My husband had done some fieldwork, and he and Einstein were talking about the fieldwork with artificial explosions, you know, to start an earthquake. . . . And Einstein said, 'What earthquake?' And Tolman said, 'Now.' And the next morning Mrs. Einstein and I went to do a little shopping, and she said, 'What do you say about our two dumbbells?'"

6.9 Aram Sahakian, general manager of the City of Los Angeles's Emergency Management Department, grew up in Beirut during the Lebanese Civil War. Everyday existence during his childhood had been food rations, sandbag walls, living amid rubble without power. Falling bombs were normal; sometimes they hit his school. "It matures you. Very quickly," Sahakian told me good-naturedly. "When I was fifteen, I felt like I was thirty years old."

To anticipate all manner of threats, but especially the Big One, Sahakian's department conducted large-scale drills at its headquarters downtown. For bunker fans, the building was beyond compare: blast-resistant exterior surfaces, emergency backup generators, reserve sewage-storage tanks, all poised on forty seismically isolated bases so it could survive a massive impact. One winter morning, city and county brass gathered for a day of pretend Armageddon. The action took place in the Main Coordination Room, a high-tech bunker ballroom straight out of a disaster movie. (The department regularly turned down film requests from Hollywood, one employee said.) There was a jumbotron, surrounded by displays. Sixteen pods were arrayed across the floor, each with half a dozen workstations clustered together and a large wide-screen monitor that would rise majestically from concealment if trouble sounded. That morning, the monitors had risen.

Employees from more than thirty agencies took part in an

eight-hour simulation. In the Joint Information Center, a large conference room overlooking the Coordination Room, more than a dozen officers from different departments—police, fire, the airport—sat at long tables, drinking coffee. No one but the simulators knew what was planned. Then a phone rang: it was Fox News, "Fox News" being one of the controllers running the simulation, wondering if the officials had heard something about a cyberattack. Soon an LAPD sergeant, playing his part, arrived with intelligence about two emergencies: a bus had exploded near City Hall, and another explosion had taken place in a residential area. After that, news filtered in about every fifteen minutes. Other incidents had occurred, in Boston and Washington. Downtown, more than a thousand people were in need of evacuation. In South L.A., some sixty-five persons needed to be moved, including thirty-five disabled children, a police officer said.

One of the information officers raised her hand. "Can we say, 'children with disabilities' instead?"

"This is the verbiage that was given to me," the officer responded sternly.

The crisis would turn out to be a multipronged siege that, in L.A., focused on the public transportation system—a cyberattack followed by a complex coordinated terrorist assault. Early in the day, one man was monitoring social media. The simulators had actually mocked up a fake version of Twitter. "We're getting people saying they're on a bus with a terrorist," he announced worriedly. He wanted to respond to the tweet and ask for details. None of us knew the scope of what was coming. How many terrorists? How many bombs? Were citizens armed and in the streets? "There's no way to private message—we'll just have to go public with it," he muttered to himself.

A good reminder that from here on out, the rough draft of history would be written on social media.

"No place on Earth offers greater security to life and greater freedom from natural disasters than Southern California," boasted the newspaper in 1934, a claim that was not only false but callous: a wildfire in Griffith Park had killed twenty-nine people a year earlier. Four years later, the Los Angeles, San Gabriel, and Santa Ana rivers all burst their banks and killed more than a hundred. More recently, in light of the Big One, emergency preparedness had become a trend in Southern California, though it was often focused on the tangible, the touchable: bug-out bags, survival knives. In 2019 Oprah put a Prepster Emergency Backpack on her list of favorite things. Preppi, the bag's maker, sent me its 3-Day Emergency Kit for review. The product description said it was designed "to fit perfectly on the bookshelf in your home or office." All I could think was, in the event of a big quake or some nuclear missiles from North Korea, wouldn't it wind up buried under a mound of paperbacks?

"Do I think Californians are doing the most they can? Probably not. But it's on the top of the minds of a lot of people I know," Jacob Margolis, the local host of *The Big One*, an earthquake podcast, told me. "There's going to be a reckoning. There will be many reckonings. And we will have to make some hard decisions. The question is, do we want to make those decisions before shit goes down? Or do we just want to wait, and it'll cost us more money down the road?"

Sahakian said it was easy to fear things like earthquakes or tsunamis for their concreteness, but what about the threat we could pose to one another when the effects of a disaster arrived downstream? Not from a lack of "social distancing," but from not knowing our neighbors' names? "Some people think you buy that five-gallon bucket from Amazon that becomes a toilet seat, and you're prepared," Sahakian said. "You're not." He encouraged people to get to know their neighbors and learn to care for them, if only out of self-interest. Community and social connectedness do not come with two-day delivery, he pointed out, and when the Big One hit, when fires stretched for blocks and the streets were ankle-deep in jagged glass, the 911 switchboard would be inundated with calls, and perhaps a child-care center somewhere would be on fire, with thirty kids trapped inside. Did anyone really think the city had enough resources to prioritize their problems in that case? "When there's a disaster, police and fire aren't first responders, they're second responders," he told me. "Make no mistake about that. First responders are a family member or a neighbor of yours."

A few weeks into the COVID-19 pandemic, I called Sahakian and caught him eating a protein bar during a break between meetings related to the city's response. The Emergency Operations Center was in full swing, and he assured me, as confident as ever, that his neighbor-helping-neighbor advice was still relevant. "Knock on your neighbor's door—do they need food? Great, get some food, leave it outside the door, let them know it's there. Helping neighbors, yes, absolutely! Just maintain that six-foot distance."

On a recent November morning, the Los Angeles Fire Department led an exercise in our neighborhood to simulate an evacuation in the event of the Big One or another emergency. Officers turned out in fire trucks. A communications squad set up a large antenna. A helicopter flew overhead—frankly, it could've been paparazzi—and the mood felt sufficiently disaster-like, yet only two neighbors emerged to inspect the commotion—a pair of men who stood around for a couple of minutes with their arms crossed, talking awkwardly about cleaning out their garages.

6.10 Northridge, the city-state's last big tremblor, was a 6.7-magnitude blind thrust earthquake that killed fifty-eight, injured nine thousand, and damaged or destroyed more than eighty-two thousand buildings in 1994. The novelist Jade Chang grew up in Northridge. "I feel a weird affinity with earthquakes," she said. "I think it's an awareness that the Earth is alive. When you've experienced a few different earthquakes and you feel the different ways the Earth can move, where it's a rolling wave or it's an up-and-down jolt—there's something fascinating about that." She laughed. "Like, all right, *We see you, we're aware of you.*"

In 1865, an earthquake shocked San Francisco, destroying City Hall. The reporter Samuel Clemens, not yet known worldwide as Mark Twain, wrote, "Every door, of every house, as far as the eye could reach, was vomiting a stream of human beings; and almost before one could execute a wink and begin another, there was a massed multitude of people stretching in endless procession down every street my position commanded. Never was solemn solitude turned teeming life quicker."

City records said that the weird old Spanish Colonial house that Rachel and I rented near the Hollywood fault rested on what the city referred to as an "earthquake-induced liquefaction area." The term *liquefied* was first used with regard to soil mechanics by Allen Hazen, an expert in hydraulics, after the failure of the Calaveras Dam near San Jose in 1918. Hazen wrote in 1920, "If the pressure of the water in the pores is great enough to carry all the load, it will have the effect of holding the particles apart and of producing a condition that is practically equivalent to that of quicksand." When we signed the lease, we knew by virtue of a little research that we'd become fault-line residents. But not that the soil beneath us could go molten.

How do you defend against quicksand?

How much longer is a place worth living in, during an epoch of fire and shakeouts and pandemics, knowing a bloodbath is coming soon to a region where small causes have such great effects?

"Between fires and earthquake, you feel much closer to nature not being a beneficent force. There's no woo-woo about it," Kit Rachlis, the former editor in chief of *Los Angeles Magazine* and *LA Weekly*, told me. "One associates New Age gauziness with California, but the flip side is that Californians are much more familiar with how violent nature can be. On the one hand is the soft, beautiful Los Angeles light. On the other are the Santa Ana winds. We have forces of nature that change people's moods— and bring fires. Crossing the street in Fort Greene, Brooklyn, or a bridge on the Seine in Paris, you just don't feel that way."

6.11 One weekend in December, the survival expert Thomas Coyne invited me to attend his annual survival class in the San Bernardino National Forest, where students went out into the woods carrying only a metal bottle and a knife. *You will leave with no food or water, and will consume only what is found,* the materials said. *Students will learn to overcome the unexpected.* "We're going to force you to problem-solve under stress so you can put that to use if you ever get in a real scenario," Coyne said. "That way you don't panic, you don't think it's hopeless."

"You know, it's not very common that people train under stress," he added. "Not at all."

It is also not very common to get a car stuck in snow in Southern California, but it can happen. At nearly seven thousand feet, about a two-hour drive east of Skid Row, the terrain was all white mountains and alpine forest. The forecast for the weekend looked grim: three days straight of rain and snow. Coyne's directions led to a dirt road high up in the mountains. Other students, also driving sedans, also stuck, were discussing what to do, until one of Coyne's instructors, Adam Mayfield, hiked out of the woods: a tall, alarmingly handsome man with an ax and several knives hanging off his belt. "Who's ready to suffer?" Mayfield said in a booming voice, then set about getting our cars properly parked.

To learn later that Mayfield, in addition to teaching survival skills, was a working Hollywood actor, a former soap opera star, really only cemented the L.A.-ness of it all.

The plan described in the preparation materials was succinct. *Day 1 is an introduction to the critical skills you will use. Days 2–3 are in the field and students will receive no outside food or water. No sleeping bags or gear allowed.* The group, mostly in their thirties and forties, included three engineers, a nurse, and a surgeon. Largely men, a few women, people who had flown in from Chicago, New York City, Detroit. The general mood was buoyant dread. About twenty people had been expected, but only thirteen showed—due to the weather conditions, Mayfield suspected. "You're going to be really challenged this weekend," he told the group. "Some of you might get dehydrated. Some of you may become mildly hypothermic." A few people laughed nervously. Mayfield added, "I *love* this."

The first day's tasks included building fires and learning how to "baton" wood, or split logs with a knife. In the afternoon, the group worked in pairs to build A-frame structures out of fallen branches, shelters we'd sleep in that night to ease into the hardship, albeit with sleeping bags. Soon, the clouds started to piss. My partner, a tech worker named Farshad, and I raced to complete our shelter, piling on a slurry of needles and branches, working by headlamps in the rain. Everyone was soaked and shivering. The temperature was in the thirties. "You can die in this kind of weather," one man muttered to himself. An hour later, he had pulled the plug. "I mean, that's a basic survival lesson, right?" he said, announcing that he was leaving. "Don't make stupid mistakes?"

Awkward silence, then Mayfield walked him out to the road and helped him get his car unstuck.

Not much sleep that night. The roof of leaves was only twelve inches from our noses. Clumps of dirt fell in my mouth. Snow mixed in with the roofing materials melted on my face. It was seven hours of claustrophobic water torture. Mostly I lay there wondering if I was making a stupid mistake.

Saturday it rained nonstop. Temperatures were in the upper thirties, low forties. Two more people dropped out, deciding they were in over their heads. The reduced band set out from camp and spent the next two hours crossing snowy hills. Even in the rain and mist, the terrain was stunning. Mayfield, smoking cigarettes like a French mountain guide, pointed out survival tricks along the way: how to purify creek water; how the bark of a willow tree can be chewed for its salicin, a chemical with properties similar to aspirin. Before the expedition left that morning, he had demonstrated how to make a fire with found materials—a branch bent into a bow, a piece of cord, a small stick for a drill, a flat piece of wood. With a couple of minutes of sawing, he suddenly had fire in his hands. It was astonishing to see, though it would be quite difficult to replicate given the conditions outside, he explained.

Eventually we reached a clearing along a ridgeline of oaks and spruce coated in fog. Farshad and I, plus a guy named David, scoured the area, searching for branches to build a shelter to survive the night. After two hours a structure was raised. After four hours, a roof and vestibule. By that point, without food or water, the group was moving slowly. Gloves, socks, and boots were soaked. The cold was inside and out. That night as we settled down, side by side, on soggy dirt and leaves, deep shivers would start in my belly and ripple to my fingers. David occasionally crawled out to do push-ups in the mud; otherwise he lay huddled. Farshad kept saying under his breath, like a death rattle, *Fuuuuuuuuuuck*. Around three in the morning, Farshad said he couldn't feel his feet anymore. His breathing sounded raggedly shallow. "This is the coldest I've ever felt in my life," he said and went out for a walk in the dark. When he got back, David worked him through some squats while I announced a new plan: We would sandwich him with our bodies, and for all our sakes the next five hours would be mandatory spooning. And it worked. After a few minutes pressed together, heat radiated at the contact points. After an hour, Farshad's breathing seemed to return to normal. By six a.m., we dragged ourselves out and did jumping jacks of joy. Others emerged from their hobbit dens and joined us. There would be more lessons throughout the day—how to build a stretcher for an injured party, how to signal for rescue—but all anyone could talk about was the thrill of surviving, of gaining the confidence to stick it out. Leaning on those around us, in the way that disaster demands.

That evening, I drove home with the windows open, guzzling coffee, thinking that human beings may be a short-sighted species when it came to planetary survival, but the corollary was that many people, in clear and present danger, wanted to help each other. And perhaps I was more resilient than I knew, though it had little to do with being tough. In the woods, hardness felt like proof of fear, whereas softness, being vulnerable, the one to extend a hand, felt incredibly empowering.

6.12 After fire, after earthquakes, came mudslides and debris flows, equally predictable and similarly destructive. During the 1934 Crescenta Valley flood, people reported a twenty-foot wall of mud and rocks that thundered out of the canyons. In March 1978 heavy rains caused twenty deaths from flash floods. And in early 2018, mudslides hospitalized some 150 people and caused nearly $200 million in property damage, mainly around Santa Barbara. Ellen DeGeneres, a local resident, covered the story on her talk show, *Ellen*, focusing on the village of Montecito, just east of where a tidal wave of mud had bulldozed the town, killed twenty-three adults and children—the oldest was eighty-nine, the youngest was three—and closed the highway for weeks after burying it under twelve feet of earth and debris.

The actor Rob Lowe, another resident, visited the show to report on the devastation. At one point during the broadcast, a large image behind his head showed a pair of thirtysome-things, a man and woman, both looking devastated. The still was from a video that had gone viral that week, about a young couple from Montecito said on social media to have lost their house and cat to the mud; who had expected to be swept away and had written "goodbye messages" to each other; who had, in the end, been evacuated by helicopter, and finally even their cat was saved. "The first responders, when I was up there, we obviously look for the people first," Lowe said, "but there are so many pets people talk about."

In the video I found online, the young woman was crying so hard she could barely speak. It seemed that at any moment she was about to be sick.

In fact, the couple captured in the video were not from Montecito, and they weren't rescued by helicopter. They never lost a house. They didn't write messages to each other saying goodbye. At the time, Lindsey Charles and Woody Thomson, newly married, were renting an apartment at the base of Laurel Canyon, where Lindsey commuted to South Central to work with special-needs students in a public school, and Woody worked in television and built guitars by hand. Months later, Lindsey told me that to know the real story, to explain why she'd been projected crying be-hind Rob Lowe's head—and why she and her husband found the viral video so embarrassing—I needed to speak to her mother.

Diana Charles, Lindsey's mom, grew up in Illinois in the 1970s. She and her husband, Steve, had moved their family west in 1990 after the family business, based in Iowa, had reached a point where Steve could mostly man-age it from his laptop. They chose Southern California for the same reason many people do: the climate, the aroma of blossoms, the hills full of Valencia trees, small creeks, and coastline oaks. "The coast curves in Santa Barbara," Diana told me. "The roads meander, they're not laid out. We're facing south, not west, and the mountains loom up. They hold us in with a feminine energy. They were kind of protecting us, in my mind." She paused. "For years, I viewed it that way."

In December 2017, just before the mudslides, the Thomas Fire engulfed the area, requiring Diana and her husband to evacuate for eleven days. Around Santa Barbara, fires were seasonal occurrences, but the Thomas Fire behaved oddly, she remembered thinking. Woody, the Charleses' son-in-law, from Santa Barbara originally—he and Lindsey had met in high school—described it as "lingering." "We've had fires in Santa Barbara every ten years," Woody said. "We've had other friends who've lost homes in other fires. This one lasted."

After the Thomas Fire, when they were finally allowed to return to their house, the feeling was joy and relief, Diana said. She hadn't known if they would have a home to return to. Also, the house was special. Diana sometimes used a wheelchair to assist with her multiple sclerosis. When she and her husband originally built their home in Montecito, they tailored it specifically to her needs, from the railings in the hallways to the height of kitchen counters. "It didn't take all my energy to get through the day, because it worked for me," she said. "It enabled me to feel freedom."

Then, on January 9, another evacuation order arrived, calling for heavy rain and potential mudslides. Diana and Steve considered leaving but decided against it. Rain on a burn area could be dangerous, they knew, but it didn't feel as threatening. The author T. C. Boyle, who lived nearby, who also didn't evacuate, explained afterward in an essay for *The New Yorker*: "Rain wasn't fire, and, like so many of my neighbors, I was suffering from disaster fatigue after more than a month of uncertainty and dislocation." At worst, Diana and Steve thought their road might be closed or their yard messed up. "Nobody thought the mountain would come down," Diana said.

Our conversation took place nearly a year later. Diana and her husband were renting a small house outside of Santa Barbara. From the end of the street you could look down the coastline and see the adjacent mountains where the sundowner winds, so-called for supposedly being at their strongest around sunset, historically descended after a long trip from the Colorado Rockies. Steve had declined to be interviewed; an hour in, Diana also seemed reluctant to speak. Then, during a quiet moment when I wasn't sure how to broach the subject, she looked up and stated, as if reading my mind, "You want to know the story of the night."

A "mudflow" or "debris flow" refers to water-soaked masses of dirt and rock that hurtle down a mountain with the destructive power of an avalanche, but in potentially more vicious fashion. A flow's liquid properties allow it to travel like a river, twisting and turning around obstacles while rapidly gaining speed. One Santa Barbara firefighter, interviewed for the *Ellen* show, pointed out that moving water six inches deep can knock a person down, twelve inches can lift a car, and twenty-four inches can move a truck. The mudflows that smashed into Montecito reached fifteen feet in height, moving at speeds of up to twenty miles an hour—meaning they'd been capable of lifting up and carrying off entire houses, and burying a highway under mud that basically became cement.

Around two a.m., rainwater gushed down the hills. Then the sky turned orange, like a citrus explosion. Instant daylight, people said. Some wondered if a bomb had gone off. What actually happened was that the debris flow had broken a gas line and the exploding methane lit up the sky, but no one knew that yet. No one knew anything. They didn't know that half an inch of water would fall in a five-minute span and the torched soil would absorb almost none of it. They didn't know that two-ton boulders would launch down steep slopes, and a river of rock and trees and even automobiles would soon dash toward them at frightening speed.

The Charleses' house, built where the mountain range leveled down to the ocean, ran in a linear fashion. At the bottom end, on the first floor, was Diana and Steve's bedroom. Going north led through a living room and kitchen to a connected three-car garage, which faced uphill. Diana and Steve were the only people in the house that night. Outside it was pounding rain. Around three in the morning Diana told Steve to fetch his phone from the living room; she could hear it pinging with alerts. Neither of them knew what was happening outside, only that the house had begun creaking. Diana followed Steve into the living room in her wheelchair. Steve opened the front door to see what was going on, then slammed it closed—their yard was a roaring river. At which point events began to quicken, Diana recalled. The earth began trembling. The walls began trembling. The house started to moan. "It became like multiple trains," she said. "It was a noise that encompassed every cell, every molecule all around you. You couldn't give it a direction, it was just this loud, loud, loud noise all around."

Then, hell. The interior door to the garage sprang open. A wall of mud came surging in. The garage doors had ruptured, and the Charleses' three-car garage now acted as a funnel. Essentially, the garage faced the mountain like an open mouth, and the mountain came rushing down its throat. "It was instantly upon us," Diana said, and described a heaving brown sea that promptly rose to her husband's waist. By that point they'd already headed back toward the bedroom; they were trying to make it to the stairs leading up to the second floor. "Luckily I was in my chair," Diana recalled, "because if I was standing, I would've been buried." Instead, the mud picked up her and her wheelchair and jammed them against the bedroom doorframe. All this occurred in a matter of seconds. The mud was throttling the room. There was so much pressure, she remembered, she could barely move, and her leg was pinned against the door. Meanwhile, the world roared, the living room heaved, their furniture and belongings started bashing into them—a couch, a chair, framed photographs—while the surge of mud rose higher, reaching Steve's chest. It was difficult to wade through the sludge. He tried to wrench Diana out of her wheelchair, but her leg was jammed. "I couldn't get out. We could not get my leg out." She remembered thinking they'd need to make the decision for Steve to leave, then he apologized, reached down, pulled her up as hard as he could—an effort that tore out part of her calf muscle, but suddenly she was free. He carried her into the bedroom and set her on the bed. Luckily, the furniture from the living room had formed a temporary dam in the doorway, so the mud in the bedroom was only up to Steve's knees. "We didn't know what was coming next," Diana remembered. "It's still pouring rain. We only knew what we knew at that instant—and we knew the water was still rushing outside." She had on a T-shirt, exercise pants, no shoes. Her leg was bleeding. The house they'd built to protect her was collapsing. They telephoned their daughters, Lindsey and her sister, and left them goodbye voicemails. (A year later, Lindsey played me the message on her phone: just a long pulse of static.) Then it was time to go. Their bedroom opened onto the yard with French doors. Steve put Diana on his back, and they headed out. The yard was a booming river channel. Even outside, the mud was up to Steve's thighs. "Steve's piggybacking me, and I'm like, 'Just go that way! Go go go!'" They headed for the woods between their house and a neighbor's. By now it was half past three in the morning, Diana guessed. "The earth was trembling. Here was mud cascading. Most people will say they remember what it smelled like, what it felt like—it's very sensory. I guess time slowed down. I remember thinking, *I know I might die here, but I never thought it would be this way.*" In the woods, Steve saw a light in the distance, a flashlight in a cottage. A small old man beckoned them inside, even offering Diana a pair of dungarees—she remembered she hadn't heard the word in such a long time—and turned around while she changed. Then another neighbor came in from the rain, a man Diana referred to as the "Gentle Giant," an enormous figure who said he knew a house nearby where they'd be safe, and they followed him out.

A little while later, Woody Thomson's phone rang in Los Angeles. He and Lindsey were asleep. The Caller ID said it was his father-in-law. Lindsey recalled waking up and hearing Woody saying, "What do you mean, the house is gone?"

In just a few hours, the flooding in Montecito would destroy sixty-five homes and damage more than four hundred. Steve and Diana were evacuated the next day by helicopter. Lindsey and Woody met them at a small airport. Along the way, they'd bought a new wheelchair at Walmart and arranged for a hotel room. For weeks, no one from the community was allowed back into the neighborhood. Search and rescue efforts involved hundreds of first responders. At the same time, a relative of Woody's heard that animal rescue groups were also involved, searching for missing pets—so she told them about Lindsey's cat, who had been living in the Charleses' house. On the seventh day after the mudflow, the cat was found. A rescuer spotted paw prints in the mud near the house, climbed in through a window, and discovered the animal covered in hardened mud. Woody and Lindsey drove to the rescue. Sure enough, there was Lindsey's cat. A woman working at the rescue asked if it would be possible to record a video to say thanks to the man who'd found their pet, and would they mind if the group posted it on Facebook to share the good news?

Two hours later Woody got a message from a friend. Was this him in this video? By that point it had around a thousand views. By the time they went to bed that night, it was closer to ten thousand. The next morning the video had gone viral; then the *Ellen* show posted it on Instagram and showed the photo of them on TV. It seemed as if every person they'd ever met began to call, Woody recalled, completely to their embarrassment. The true story was that when Steve called Woody, saying the house was gone, they thought they might die, Lindsey had leaped out of bed to pack a bag and her body failed. Complete collapse. It had never happened before. Her thoughts were lucid, she was grabbing a pair of sneakers; then she overheard Woody say something on the phone to her parents—whom she might never see again, she was realizing—and all her muscles failed in unison and she fell over. It continued for several minutes. Get up, collapse, get up, collapse. Finally she was able to steel her mind and leave, and for the next seven days she didn't cry once, Lindsey said, even though her childhood home was gone, she had almost lost her parents, and people she and Woody had known had died in the disaster. But then a nice lady asked to make a video about her old cat, and tears burst out, and they were of a similar nature to her muscular system the night her father had called on the phone: completely out of her control.

A year later, Lindsey and Woody moved to Santa Barbara to be closer to their families. Diana told me that she and her husband weren't sure where they'd go next. Their small community had worked together in the aftermath to recover and heal in ways she found extraordinary. And she knew they were fortunate in ways others were not; their family business and savings protected them, affording them privilege that many people didn't have. "We have our story, but people died," she said toward the end of our interview. "I know what that sound was. I know what that smell was. I don't know how anyone makes peace with that."

In Montecito, when I visited, many roads remained closed for rebuilding. Lindsey and Woody drove me to where her family's house once stood. On the trees was a distinct waterline that showed how high the mud had been, maybe seven feet off the ground; and the actual ground under our feet was the flow itself, hardened like rock. Still, on every block were signs of reconstruction. Lindsey said she knew a real estate agent who'd received calls on the morning of the slides from clients abroad who heard about the disaster and wanted to buy properties unseen, in cash. Even a year later, she seemed flabbergasted, shaking her head. "It was a once-in-a-lifetime event," she said, "but one that has happened before. It will happen again."

6.13 "It was like those days when you heard a thunderstorm coming and there was the waiting silence and then the faintest pressure of the atmosphere as the climate blew over the land in shifts and shadows and vapors. And the change pressed at your ears and you were suspended in the waiting time of the coming storm. You began to tremble. The sky was stained and colored; the clouds were thickened; the mountains took on an iron taint. The caged flowers blew with faint sighs of warning. You felt your hair stir softly. Somewhere in the house the voice-clock sang, 'Time, time, time, time . . .' ever so gently, no more than water tapping on velvet" (Ray Bradbury, *The Martian Chronicles*).

LESSON 7

There's Nothing to See Here, and That's the Point

7.0   When they were born, Bay Davis once said, a pastor told their mother she was pregnant with a prophet. Named Mike at birth and later named Bay, at times they had gone by, or referred to themselves online as, They Davis and Hood Profet, a poet, a shape-shifter, a tattoo artist. Brought up in the hustle, learning their mother's path, the two of them had raised each other around Los Angeles, Davis said. One night staying in a mansion. One night in a motel. One morning washing up and changing clothes in a department store bathroom. More recently, they might wear a pair of gold nose rings and multiple sets of hoops, a white dress or a pantsuit and pumps, or a Chicago Bulls jersey over camouflage pants. Very little about them was not molten in some manner. Though, if they wore their hair short, they presented Brown, they said. If they grew it out, people saw Black. "I know what it is to have a Brown mother and be a Black person," they told me. "It took me a really long time to learn how to navigate that."

Around the time they were twelve, Davis recalled, their mother moved them and their sister into a two-story house on a pretty, tree-lined street just south of L.A. Memorial Coliseum, the home of Trojans football. A few years later the family was served an eviction notice, part of a local trend: apartment buildings and houses near the University of Southern California fluttering with eviction notices as units got flipped—what some called gentrification, some called redevelopment, and some called economic ethnic cleansing. As Hood Profet, known for writing poetry that was often about gentrification and race, they had garnered a large following on social media—so to help out their family and raise money, they inaugurated an event at the house called Porch Poetry. Davis and friends would read poems from the stoop. Anyone else who wanted to read, or just hang out and listen, could pay five dollars, or nothing, if they couldn't afford it. The idea came from a sense of frustration, they said. "How do I resist gentrification in my community? We were like, we can't do nothing."

For the first Porch Poetry they set out a dozen chairs. Almost nobody came. A few weeks and iterations later, by nine p.m. on a warm summer night, more than a hundred people were crowded in the darkness, waiting patiently, with dozens more standing at the gate.

7.1 From founding to present, the city-state has been divided between the powerful and the powerless, the haves and have-nots, those who move through halls of authority hoarding dispensations and those who, for all intents and purposes, are stuck on blocks that feel more like the industrial Midwest than any Californian dream.

In the city-state of America, perhaps the city-state of globalism, if there was a single story I uncovered in all my traversing and interviewing, talking to social workers, salsa makers, luxury concierges—listening for a single narrative to connect the ten-million-plus together—the story wasn't fire or homelessness, and definitely not the movies. The story was inequality.

7.2 Under lights at Porch Poetry, on either flank of the stoop, were bunches of yellow balloons. Concessions were served, a DJ played hip-hop, a pop-up shop sold handmade shirts. The crowd was almost entirely Black and Brown, mostly young. A fashionable T-shirt for sale said POETRY NOT POVERTY / POEMS NOT PRISONS.

The neighborhood, a few blocks south of Exposition Park, buzzed with low-key volume. Neighbors hung out in the shadows. Couples embraced, dawdling around cars. At Porch Poetry, person after person stood up to read poems about broken hearts and broken lives, real activists versus "hashtag activists," and the cost of existing in colored skin in America. A young Black woman read a poem about her cousin being killed by a white man, which she struggled to understand. It wasn't Black-on-Black crime, but why should Black-on-Black crime make sense? A helicopter whopped-whopped overhead, and she paused. People snapped their fingers in encouragement. Her poem ended, "I've been craving substance, something resembling justice / but somehow it always seems like I just missed the freedom train."

Southern Los Angeles, or South L.A., as developers called it in lieu of South Central (one woman in the audience wore a T-shirt that said IT'S CALLED SOUTH CENTRAL), was undergoing rapid change. New transit. New stadiums. New (unaffordable) housing. New (white) faces. Several people read poems about learning that "home" could become a vanished place, about their specific neighborhoods—Inglewood,

Leimert Park—being stolen out from under them. "In the wee hours of the night," L.A.-born Paul Beatty wrote in *The Sellout*, "after the community boards, homeowner associations, and real estate moguls banded together and coined descriptive names for nondescript neighborhoods, someone would bolt a large glittery Mediterranean-blue sign high up on a telephone pole. And when the fog lifted, the residents of the soon-to-be gentrified blocks awoke to find out they lived in Crest View, La Cienega Heights, or Westdale. Even though there weren't any topographical features like crests, views, heights, or dales to be found within ten miles."

In fact, that night would be Porch Poetry's last, at least in that location. The landlord had ordered it shut down, Davis told me a few weeks later at a nearby Starbucks. "When you hustle, you can be rich one day and have nothing the next day. Literally everything is come and go," they said. By that point, their mother and sister had moved to Nevada, and they'd invited friends to move in, to make the apartment a home for queer Brown and Black kids for as long as it lasted. In an interview I found online, from the website L.A. Taco, Davis said to a reporter, "If I don't build a consistent space that can sustain, then what am I doing for people?"

"My life has been built on instability," they told me, resignedly. "Part of me loves that shit."

The blue sky outside the coffee shop was empty, shaming any clouds. In a room of white and Asian kids all in identical fleece and jeans, Davis had cut a figure. They were tall and slender, in a towering headwrap, wearing almost a dozen golden rings that they slowly removed and stacked on the table. "Not that I'm comfortable, but sometimes I crave it—chaos. It's how I learned love," they said. "The other side of this is, I've become super into routine. I make homes everywhere I go. Even just on a day-to-day level, I wake up and do the same exact thing every morning, listen to the same songs every morning. I need stability. When I was homeless, it's like, 'Yeah I'm showering in the bathroom of a fucking Walmart, but I know I'm doing this first, doing this next, I'm playing this song and then doing this.' Because without that I lose my fucking mind."

In the time spent working on this book, when I thought about how people lived in the city-state, how many different versions of Los Angeles a person might contain, Davis was often the person who came to mind as someone representing L.A.'s finer qualities: resilience, diversity, creativity in the face of attack. Perhaps a prophet but also a medium, a hieroglyph. Basically, the best representative of the city-state I had met.

7.3 To appreciate inequality in Los Angeles, to grasp the rules and how they operated in realpolitik—because cities are never just cities, towns not just towns, neighborhoods not just blocks and parks but also instruments for discrimination—an observer might turn to the laws of motion.

Growing up in the city-state, Erin Aubry Kaplan knew that the most important rules were not always written down. You don't go west of Main Street. You don't go south of Slauson. You don't go north of the 10. Growing up in South Central and Inglewood, these were the boundaries of her childhood. Today, she goes wherever she likes, and when she was in Venice, Kaplan explained, she was Venetian. If she spent time in Larchmont, she was part of Larchmont. As a journalist, Kaplan had covered Black Los

Angeles for years at the *Los Angeles Times* and *LA Weekly*; more recently, she wrote columns for *The New York Times*. But Los Angeles County, all of it, was hers no matter where she went. Walking her dogs in El Segundo—originally a company town for Standard Oil, now a mostly white beachside community near LAX—Kaplan became part of El Segundo. "I've been racially profiled in El Segundo, but I continue to go down there," she said. "I claim El Segundo, dammit!"

"California is the greatest state for the negro," Jefferson L. Edmonds, editor of *The Liberator*, declared in 1902. Kaplan's father, the activist and journalist Larry Aubry, arrived in Los Angeles as a child in the 1940s during a wave of Black migration. Back then, she explained, the city seemed to many African American families like a golden opportunity, or at least a brighter one than many found in the South or the Midwest. Though when her father's family arrived, the social order in place was pretty similar to that in the rest of the country. Persistent racism. Widespread segregation. A 2007 profile of her father noted that at Fremont High School, where he'd been a student, "in 1947, blacks were hung in effigy. Posted signs proclaimed, 'No n——,' and, later, blacks were barred from residing in—even entering—Inglewood." Still, there was room for achievement, for stability, for some. "This Los Angeles produced architect Paul Williams, Nobel Prize winner Ralph Bunche, Mayor Tom Bradley, the Liberty Savings and Loan Company, the Golden State Mutual Life Insurance Company," the historian Kevin Starr noted in *Golden Dreams: California in an Age of Abundance, 1950–1963*. "You had a shot," Kaplan said.

"Any seed or insect or lizard or mammal that found itself

in L.A. had to believe that there was a chance to thrive" (Walter Mosley, *Blonde Faith*).

And still, for many new Black arrivals, Los Angeles wasn't Joan Didion's tabula rasa but a place built on the United States' deep racist rot. The housing authority and private industry, unified in redlining, called Black neighborhoods "blighted districts." Beaches and swimming pools were segregated. African Americans were locked out of neighborhoods, social clubs, careers. Homes were bombed and burned. Bodies were brutalized by the police. Sugar Hill, one of the city's most prosperous Black middle-class areas, was destroyed in 1954 for the Santa Monica Freeway. Basically, L.A. was a profoundly unequal society designed to benefit whites, with precedents big and small. Charlotta Bass, editor and publisher of the Black newspaper *The California Eagle*, noted in 1938, "Here in Los Angeles, the Negro domestic worker is becoming one of the most brazenly exploited group of laboring groups. The plight of those cooks, waitresses, and general housework employees who have been forced to accept starvation wages from individual employers has long been known and lamented."

By the 1970s, when Kaplan's parents bought a house in Inglewood, the neighborhood had become synonymous with white flight. In 1965, what some called the Watts Rebellion—what Dr. Martin Luther King Jr. called "the beginning of a stirring of those people in our society who have been bypassed by the progress of the past decade"— was labeled widely as riot and mayhem and hellfire: several days of combustion and violence, with almost four thousand people arrested, more than two dozen killed. A *Life* magazine photo spread from that time: "Out of a Cauldron of Hate." And yet the federal government's Kerner Commission report, the product of a seven-month study into the event's instigation, would blame what happened in Watts almost completely on white society. "What white Americans have never fully understood—but what the Negro can never forget—is that white society is deeply implicated in the ghetto. White institutions created it, white institutions maintain it, and white society condones it."

In Inglewood, one of Kaplan's neighbors had been the first Black family on the block. Every day, Kaplan said, the neighbor watched as another homeowner, a white man, came outside and refused to say hello. Instead he'd stare at her from his porch, demanding loudly, "Why are you here?"

A few months after Kaplan and I talked, I discovered a sociological examination of an unidentified part of Los Angeles, *The Changing Urban Neighborhood* (1929) by Bessie Averne McClenahan. In one section, "The Negro Invasion," interviews conducted with white residents were excerpted. One woman said, "When I took my son out of the ___ School, he said, 'But, mother, why are we going away?' I told him because there were so many Negroes there and he said: 'But, mother, they are all right and they are nice little children.' You see he had already taken the wrong attitude." Another woman commented, "I like the colored people, they are excellent people but they do not know their place. It is one thing for me to invite the children of my colored woman who has worked for me for twenty years to come over and see our Christmas tree, but what do they do but the next week turn around and invite my children to come and see their tree. That shows how well they know their places, as if I would allow my children to go down there to 'N——' town to see their tree!"

Kaplan and her late husband bought a house in Inglewood in 2004. When she and I spoke fifteen years later, the neighborhood was selling fast, and the appeal was obvious: a sunny corner of groomed gardens near the ocean and the airport, with Mediterranean breezes and cool nights. Black neighbors were sending each other emails, Kaplan said, urging one another not to sell out. *The only thing we can do is not sell. Don't sell!* In part because, she suggested, though high prices were tempting, those who stuck around might enjoy certain benefits: a new rail line, new shopping options. And not all the buyers were white. One new Black owner had moved recently from Chicago with his girlfriend. He told me he loved it for the sunshine, the ease of getting around—and had I noticed how people just let you merge into lanes on the freeway? "I've just never been so happy," he said. "Like, every day I'm happy."

Still, Kaplan's neighbors were selling. Black citizens once constituted almost a fifth of L.A.'s population. Recent numbers were less than 10 percent, thanks to deindustrialization, government disinterest, the upwardly mobile moving out. And still the downwardly immobile in South Central dealt with drug addiction, street violence, police terror—not to mention under-policing, as the local journalist Jill Leovy argued in *Ghettoside: A True Story of Murder in America* (2015), which showed the LAPD's inability to punish the murderers of Black citizens—indeed, its historical interest in *not* punishing their killers—to be a primary cause of regional violence. "Take a bunch of teenage boys from the whitest, safest suburb in America and plunk them down in a place where their friends are murdered and they are constantly attacked and threatened," Leovy wrote. "Signal that no one cares, and fail to solve murders. Limit their options for escape. Then see what happens."

Much had changed. Much had not. In 2020, during the Black Lives Matter protests following the police murders of George Floyd and other Black Americans, a local white councilman, who was also a thirty-year veteran of the LAPD, suggested attacking protesters with liquid feces. "Mobilize the septic tank trucks, put a pressure cannon on em . . . hose em down . . . the end."

The great American dream, in Kaplan's view, boiled down to mobility. It was the ability to go where you wanted, live where you wanted, stroll wherever you liked without fear of police and their septic cannons, white women and their phones. "This is a capitalist game. This is an economics game," Kaplan said. "Unfortunately, race and economics are so closely tied together, unless you fight economics with economics, I don't know how this changes." She had a theory that gangsta rap, a local invention, had partly derived from Black people being able to visit places like Santa Monica but not own property, and I was reminded of a clipping I found, from Santa Monica's *Weekly Interpreter* in 1922: "Negroes, we don't want you here; now and forever this is to be a white man's town."

So Kaplan would stay in Inglewood, document, defend, remember. Her story, she told me, drew from many of the worlds the city-state contained: African American L.A., artist L.A., Creole L.A., intellectual L.A. Most of all, freak L.A., the freakiness of people who defied expectations. Maybe there wasn't a single shared place in the city-state, but perhaps there was a shared dream, however unrealistic. To mingle on the beach. To claim any street as your own. "The ideal that my family came here for," she said, "is the great American ideal: living together."

7.4 From *Empire of Signs* (1970) by Roland Barthes: "Quadrangular, reticulated cities (Los Angeles, for instance) are said to produce a profound uneasiness. They offend our synesthetic sentiment of the City, which requires that any urban space have a center to go to, to return from, a complete site to dream of and in relation to which to advance or retreat; in a word, to invent oneself."

From Carl Anthony, president of Earth Island Institute, during a forum in 1996 on the future of American cities: "The question is: Do people have the right to choose to be racist, and then to dominate the political life of the nation because they have built their lives around that choice?"

From Hebrews 10:39: "But we do not belong to those who shrink back and are destroyed, but to those who have faith and are saved."

7.5 In a region of riptides and highway driving, laws of motion sometimes deal in life and death. In 2020, during the novel coronavirus pandemic, those who could afford to work from home stayed inside, while others delivered packages, fought wildfires, bagged groceries, and then rode home on crowded buses. D. J. Waldie, the nondriving poet of Lakewood, once wrote, "We don't connect otherwise, you who drive and we who are driven. Despite more than 2,500 buses on L.A. streets and more than 18,500 stops in the Metro system, public transit is almost invisible to the 90% of L.A. that prefers a car. Which leaves the transit-dependent locked in a system that provides a ride but not much ease or respect."

When we remember the city-state icon O. J. Simpson, what do we remember most? The running back, the escape, the absolution. Football field, freeway, acquittal. "Of all the specific liberties which may come into our minds when we hear the word 'freedom,' freedom of movement is historically the oldest and also the most important" (Hannah Arendt, *Men in Dark Times*).

Those citizens who were the least mobile, needless to say, were the men and women, mostly men, locked in cages. The United States had long imprisoned more citizens than any other country, and inside the U.S., the city-state caged the most. L.A.'s jail system was the world's largest, with many cells filled with the mentally ill, and many citizens who simply couldn't make bail. In Kelly Lytle Hernández's *City of Inmates: Conquest, Rebellion, and the Rise of Human Caging in Los Angeles, 1771–1965*, Los Angeles's emergence as America's "carceral capital" was part of a long act of conquest, and this dated back to when the city was mostly white. "By 1910, when white men comprised nearly 100 percent of the local jail population, Los Angeles operated one of the largest jail systems in the country." Though by the 1950s, when L.A.'s jail system was the country's biggest, its inhabitants were increasingly Black, and the population was growing. According to *Golden Gulag*, Ruth Wilson Gilmore's study of California prisons, between 1982 and 2000 the state prisoner population expanded almost 500 percent, "even though the crime rate peaked in 1980 and declined, unevenly but decisively, thereafter." Most of the prisoners were from cities, especially Los Angeles. Neighborhoods were hollowed out, families demolished. Disproportionate incarceration meant that young Black men, by and large, were disappeared, subjected to the county jails' "force first" approach of control—a system to crush and punish, and destroy lives inside and out. Whereas in many parts of Los

Angeles, the police and prisons barely figured. And when people on those blocks expressed shock to me at the notion of "defunding" the police state or "abolishing" prisons—those concepts of demilitarizing cops, allocating funding to social services, finding alternative solutions to our extraordinarily expensive and ineffective method of fighting crime—they didn't seem to realize they lived in neighborhoods where cops and jails barely played a role, where "defund the police" was already the norm.

In fact, the militarization of American policing is often credited to the city-state, to the Los Angeles Police Department, whose midcentury use of SWAT teams inspired law enforcement nationwide.

Finally, if freed from prison, a person was still pinned down. A recent report in *The Economist* about California's alarming rate of poverty—from 2015 to 2017, 19 percent of Californians were poor, while the national average was around 14 percent—found that the state "has been more enthusiastic than most states in passing laws restricting what ex-convicts can do. A staggering 4,800 laws prevent former felons getting public housing, or licenses to work as anything from a car mechanic to a nurse."

Terrence, a thirtysomething white guy from SoCal who I met in the course of interviews, described what it was like the first time he was processed for drug possession in the Men's Central Jail. A windowless concrete dungeon, the jail had been plagued by a "long-entrenched culture of savage deputy-on-inmate violence," according to the county jail facilities' court-ordered monitor, the ACLU. To start, Terrence was put in a pen for six or seven hours with eighteen other men. Benches were only a few inches wide, to keep the men from sleeping. Most of the men were in for drugs, Terrence recalled, a few for domestic assault. Food was peanut butter packets. One guy came up to him making slurping sounds, like Hannibal Lecter, saying, "Ooh yeah, suck that down." Eventually the men were photographed and fingerprinted. Rooms were windowless and freezing, air-conditioned to maybe sixty degrees, he recalled. Terrence watched one jailer get his shoes shined by an inmate. Saw another officer beat the shit out of an inmate, kicking and punching him while he sat cowering; another inmate explained that the attack was because the man was a pedophile, supposedly. Next, the inmates were instructed to strip while one of the guards berated them for twenty minutes—"you could tell he really enjoyed it, yelling at us," Terrence said—then a cold shower followed by more barking before they were given jumpsuits and sent to their cells. Terrence was released about thirty-six hours later after a friend posted bail. He knew he'd been one of the lucky ones—white dude, first-time offender, able-bodied. "Even still, it fucks with your mind," he said. "I honestly started thinking maybe I'd be stuck here for the next couple months."

7.6 Bay Davis invited me to a ball. The night was cloudy, with a big moon. Around eleven, in a smoky room on the top floor of the club, the crowd was mostly young men, Brown and Black, dancing to very loud rap. Some were poised. Some looked like it was their first time in high heels. A pair of young men in lace shifts danced closely while a pair of young women gripped the hems of each other's tops so tightly they drew smiles from onlookers. Around midnight, a runway formed. One by one, people catwalked, duckwalked, acrobatically collapsed, to eruptions of applause. One man, accessorized with a tennis racquet, paid tribute to Serena Williams. A short woman, done up like Elvira, made a floor show out of demonstrating that she wore no underwear, receiving loud applause. Eventually Davis emerged, twirling slowly as the crowd parted, looking like a cross between Madonna and *the* Madonna—blue dress, blond wig, a crown of spikes that propped up a large cloud of veil—and the crowd gazed, sighed, and screamed.

Gradually the runway folded in on itself, and people resumed dancing like at any party, spinning out in gyres. People got drunk. Davis exited through a door for the fire escape and disappeared before I could interview them, at least thank them for the invitation. Outside, the bass from the club sounded like a heartbeat. The night was misty. Any cars driving below looked like they were cutting through fog, cruising by like ships.

"Once, it was like seeing the night for the very first time, only someone dangled black ice cubes in front of my eyes. Each street, each story melted on a page . . ." (Marisela Norte, "Lost in Los (Angeles)").

7.7 When Davis visited other states to perform or conduct workshops on college campuses, they often traveled, like tens of millions of others, through the city-state's great people mover: Los Angeles International Airport. Operating since 1928, LAX is a city-state unto itself. More than five square miles, it has its own SWAT team, its own anti-terrorism intelligence unit. It has its own theme song, "L.A. International Airport" (the only airport I could find with an official song), performed by the '70s country music star Susan Raye. Jackie Collins reportedly once said, "Flying in at night is just an orgasmic thrill," echoing a quote from Eleanor Roosevelt that

I found in David Kipen's *Dear Los Angeles*, where she said that the most impressive time to fly into Los Angeles was "when all the lights are on and the city lies below you like a multi-colored heap of jewels."

According to the newspaper, on the Fourth of July, pilots in the city-state often steeped their descents and take-offs to avoid the sporadic gunfire of people celebrating.

The experience prior to or post-flying was decidedly less orgasmic. For nearly everyone, travel through LAX was a trial. It was the realm, as Dante wrote, "of those who have rejected spiritual values by yielding to bestial appetites or violence, or by perverting their human intellect to fraud or malice against their fellowmen," feelings not unfamiliar to drivers of the airport's inner rings. Then came baggage check, up to an hour of queuing, and finally security, which, for the least privileged, least validated, was yet another endurance test, followed by a long walk to the gate. Making it not ludicrous for a traveler going through LAX, in some scenarios, to consider leaving home half a day or a full day before their trip.

But for those who could afford to experience less stress, the city-state within the city-state offered a semisecret gate: not far from the main terminals, the "Private Suite" was a hole in the traveler's space-time continuum. "It typically takes 2200 footsteps from car seat to plane seat. For members of The Private Suite, it's 70 footsteps," the company that manages it advertised. Basically, it was a private entrance to the airport. For an admission fee of about $3,500, a person could drive up to an unlabeled guardhouse and be escorted into a single-story row of suites and rooms where the wealthy sipped Sancerre, perhaps used the spa, then were driven across the tarmac in a BMW to board at their leisure. "Southern California, I found, is a veritable paradise of statuspheres," Tom Wolfe wrote in *The Pump House Gang*. At LAX, the Private Suite was about as status-y as it got, if barely known.

"There were great silent estates, with twelve-foot walls and wrought-iron gates and ornamental hedges; and inside, if you could get inside, a special brand of sunshine, very quiet, put up in noise-proof containers just for the upper classes" (Raymond Chandler, *Farewell, My Lovely*).

The suite's creator was Gavin de Becker. He was the author of the bestselling book *The Gift of Fear: Survival Signals That Protect Us from Violence*, though he was probably better known, through his security company, for handling the safekeeping of some of the world's wealthiest individuals, including the wealthiest at the time: De Becker was the one who helped Amazon's Jeff Bezos investigate a potential blackmail scheme attempted by *The National Enquirer* in 2019. When we spoke, De Becker said that the Private Suite benefited all L.A. flyers, not just its customers. Consider the celebrity problem. Now famous people could pay to avoid paparazzi stress, which meant that the airport—and the everyday traveler—would suffer less of the commotion and security drain that came when famous faces passed through regular doors. "Seventy-five million people move through LAX every year, and all of them are in an absolute prison," he said.

As someone born and raised in Los Angeles, De Becker once knew the city-state as a place in which to be trapped. By the time he was ten years old, he'd lived in ten places. "Before I was thirteen, I saw a man shot, I saw another beaten and kicked to unconsciousness, I saw a friend struck near lethally in the face and head with a steel rod," he wrote in *The Gift of Fear*. The book detailed how De Becker's mother regularly beat him and his sister and also shot his stepfather; she killed herself when de Becker was sixteen. "I grew up on welfare and food stamps," he told me. "Three of us kids raised by a single mother who was also a heroin addict. The only reason I had a shot at success was that I wasn't Black [in the United States]. If there'd been one more disadvantage put on me, I'm dead."

The book was, in part, about how de Becker had developed the prevailing terror of his childhood into a method of self-protection, retooling fear into something useful, even measured. It recalled a passage from *Helter Skelter*, the book by Vincent Bugliosi and Curt Gentry about L.A. in the wake of the Manson Family murders in 1969: "In two days one Beverly Hills sporting goods store sold 200 firearms; prior to the murders, they averaged three or four a day. Some of the private security forces doubled, then tripled, their personnel. Guard dogs, once priced at $200, now sold for $1,500; those who supplied them soon ran out. Locksmiths quoted two-week delays on orders."

About a week after my interview with de Becker, Rachel and I drove through the Private Suite's special gate; she was flying to visit a friend, and de Becker had voided the fee. A valet parked our Honda in a row that featured a Porsche, a Bentley, and a pair of Teslas. Inside the suite, furnishings suggested the love child of a luxury hotel and a pharmacy, stocked with any medications or accessories a traveler might need. Miniature refrigerators were filled with small bottles of French wine. Jets and service vehicles lumbered past the windows. If there'd been time, Rachel might have ordered in a pedicure or lunch from Beverly Hills or a Double-Double from In-N-Out—she'd only started to explore the offerings, when the telephone rang and a gentle voice informed her it was time for her to "be moved." A moment later her valet arrived and escorted her to a security room where the Private Suite's own TSA inspectors passed her bag through an X-ray machine; then a silver BMW drove her across the tarmac and parked under the wing of her plane, where another man met her, carried her bag up the stairs, and passed her off to a woman who escorted her to her seat in the otherwise empty cabin.

When we first arrived, Rachel's valet had given her the option of boarding first, last, or whenever (nothing said status in air travel so much as boarding when you liked). "It's a nice ride in all senses," Rachel texted me dryly from her seat in coach.

De Becker no longer lived in Los Angeles, for multiple reasons, he said. For him, the city-state, a metaphor he found accurate, was a dangerous case example in the tragedy that was income inequality, and the gentry in the hills either didn't know or didn't care. "Most people in Beverly Hills or Brentwood, they don't know shit about it. They haven't been [to Downtown] in fifteen years, if they've ever been down there. They don't have any idea what's going on." De Becker knew poverty, violence, catastrophe, all of which was why, if the United States were to survive what lay ahead, he favored a universal basic income (UBI), a periodic cash payment sent to all citizens as a way to stabilize society against sudden hardship. "If we don't do UBI or something like it, we're looking at violence," De Becker told me. What definitely loomed, from his point of view, was the climate crisis, with waves of climate refugees banging on the gates, not to mention industry automation, economic stratification. "There's not enough protection to make it work for the wealthy," he said, "when we'll have all these people who have homes and families but don't have a job anymore."

7.8 Deep into my work on this book, the newspaper published an article about the lives of ride-share drivers who were homeless and slept in their cars. It shocked me that there were enough homeless ride-share drivers to warrant an article, but of course there were. As one man explained, if a night was good, he'd pay to stay in one of the all-night Koreatown spas that allowed overnight guests, where he would see other ride-share drivers entering the spa "with the same look of shame on their face." I stared at those words a long time, a sense of despair creeping into my fingers, and typed out a list of questions in a rush:

> Do the non-rich know they're hindered by the success
> of the wealthy?
> For Porsche-driving landlords, what does a quiet
> conscience cost?
> What will a revolution in the city-state even look like?

Political rallies and marches often arose Downtown around City Hall, then dispersed. "If one took over some public square, some urban open space in Los Angeles, who would know?" Charles W. Moore, dean of the Yale School of Architecture, once said. "A march on City Hall would be inconclusive. The heart of the city would have to be sought elsewhere. The only hope would seem to be to take over the freeways." The idea being to stop in place an Angeleno conditioned to mobility—to halt the freeway for an hour during someone's commute, in the manner of France's gilets jaunes—which would tear up the social contract faster than any apocalyptic inferno. In fact, many groups have done this over the years: stopping the freeway traffic in support of Black Lives Matter, or Armenia during its conflict with Azerbaijan, or to protest President Trump. One man, who "roadblocked" in 1990 to protest the Gulf War, later sent a letter to the newspaper expressing remorse. "Looking back on my experience with civil disobedience, I wonder how many workers were made late to their jobs, how many pregnant women may have been unduly stressed by the delay in traffic, how many emergency room professionals may have missed the opportunity to mitigate suffering among my fellow community members?" In contrast, during the 2020 protests following the death of George Floyd, when a human barricade stopped traffic on the 101, one man told a radio reporter, "We took the freeway, and that's always strategic. Because the freeway represents what created segregated communities: white flight and redlining. What separates the suburbs and the ghetto or the 'hood.' What has created desperate economic conditions for our communities. We're saying: the suburbs are going to hear from us. We're all connected."

During those months of protests and marches, I often thought again of those homeless ride-share drivers, by day shuttling people to wherever they were headed, by night trapped inside their cars. Police, prisons, poverty—for all of our means of motion, where were we going? Was the city-state's story less narrative, more loop?

7.9   One afternoon around Thanksgiving, twenty minutes north of Downtown, in the foothills of the gray-blue San Gabriels, the rocket scientist Marleen Martinez Sundgaard tried to explain to me how she and her team had re-created a version of Mars on Earth with rakes, augmented reality headsets, and a lot of crushed garnet.

Five days later, NASA's InSight lander would aspire to reach Elysium Planitia, a wide plain astride the Martian equator, with a goal to map the planet's guts in three dimensions. But first InSight needed to land safely, ideally on a piece of alien landscape as flat as any Los Angeles parking lot. Sundgaard worked in a large hangar at NASA's Jet Propulsion Laboratory (JPL) in La Cañada Flintridge, above Pasadena. As InSight's lead test-bed engineer, Sundgaard specialized in the landing spot. Petite, in her thirties, with long, dark hair and a scientist's slightly distracted manner, she worked most days ankle-deep in an expensive sandbox that simulated the Red Planet's surface conditions. Assuming that InSight touched down safely, Sundgaard and her team, in order to prevent any extremely expensive snafus, would study its camera feeds to create a near-perfect simulation here on Earth of the terrain so they could repeatedly practice the deployment and calibration of the lander's instruments before actually using them in space.

Walking me around the JPL, Sundgaard wore limited-edition Vans with the NASA logo on the side. She'd snagged them online just before they sold out, she said proudly. Regarding the mission, she was nervous, anxious, randomly nauseous. Other scientists described similar reactions—only 40 percent of previous Mars landings had succeeded—but Sundgaard was something of an anomaly in their company. First of all, a woman. Second, a Latina woman. But also one who, as a team leader at NASA, had basically reached her position from another galaxy—her roots being not Los Angeles, but Los Ángeles, a Mexican village. Sundgaard was the daughter and granddaughter of migrant farmers. Born in the States, she had been made to go out into the fields at a young age, not so much to work, she told me, but to know her family's sacrifices. For five bucks and twenty-five cents an hour, she would rise at five a.m. to sharpen hoes, don large rubber boots, head out to pick and clean; anytime she nicked a single plant, she got in trouble. "[My parents] didn't want me to grow up thinking I get all of this for free," she said. "It's not free. You have to work for everything." But Sundgaard had felt destined for other things. She'd been about five years old, she recalled, when she first told her mother she wanted to be an astronaut.

7.10 The 1959 children's book *About Missiles and Men* begins, "Many men have worked many years to make today's missiles. Many more men will work many more years making more and better missiles. Here you may read about some of these men. Maybe one of them is your father or your uncle. Maybe one of these men lives next door to you. Maybe you will be one of these men someday."

Around the time of the space race, 60 percent of America's biggest aerospace companies were based in Southern California. Recently, after a falling-off, the aerospace industry again pulses: SpaceX in Hawthorne, Virgin Orbit in Long Beach, a company in Moorpark developing a flying motorcycle powered by jet engines. Perhaps a bigger surprise is how many employees are women, particularly in technical areas. For InSight, half of the core entry, descent, and landing (EDL) team were women. Broadly, the number of female engineers working in aerospace remains small, but the historical contributions of female mathematicians are becoming better known, and the progress from previous years is striking, both in figures and tone. In 1962, Werner von Braun, the former SS officer who became the public face of modern American rocketry, was asked if NASA would ever employ women astronauts. Indeed, he said, on a future mission "we're reserving 110 pounds of payload for recreational equipment."

In school Sundgaard had been known for being good at math and science. One day in middle school her principal asked her out of the blue, "Are you smart?" When she said yes, he asked her to follow him to his office, where he gave her an application to Space Camp, run by the U.S. Space & Rocket Center in Alabama. Sundgaard was elated; she'd seen Space Camp on TV. She took the application home, arduously wrote out the personal essay, and won a spot. Then someone at the camp told her she was probably too short to be a rocket pilot; she should focus on becoming a systems lead instead. So that's what she did.

Twenty-four hours before InSight was expected to land, I reached out to see how Sundgaard was doing. Nervous, excited, a little scared, she said. "I'm trying to keep my mind on things like the test bed, and our readiness to support surface operations. That's all I can do at this point." On the day of, the landing was broadcast live on the radio. I caught it driving home from the library. The final moments, the "seven minutes of terror," had long, tense silences between phrases like "heat shield separation" and "altitude convergence," until finally, the countdown: *Gravity turn, altitude 400 meters . . . 300 meters . . . 200 meters . . . 80 meters . . . 60 meters . . . 50 meters, constant velocity . . . 37 meters . . . 30 meters . . . 20 meters . . . 17 meters, standing by for touchdown . . . Touchdown confirmed!*

Mission Control erupted with applause. The car next to me at a stoplight honked twice. I rolled down my window to share in the good news, but the guy had simply bumped his horn by accident.

A week earlier, I'd asked Sundgaard—who grew up both in the United States and Mexico, with so much of her life in motion—was the American dream still attainable? Was it a moon shot like the Apollo program or more like an episode of *Star Trek*, a nostalgic fantasy? Oh, definitely still attainable, Sundgaard thought. People who declared it dead, she felt, had probably experienced some version of it, even a failed version of it, but they didn't know *none* of it. "If you're constantly drinking water and you know the taste of water, and water keeps you alive, you don't know what it's like to not be able to quench your thirst," she said. "You don't know what it's like to be thirsty all the time."

7.11 During the course of this book being written, the violent deaths of three men shook the city-state like successive quakes.

Ermias Joseph Asghedom, age thirty-three, was killed in the parking lot of a strip mall he owned. Famous as Nipsey Hussle, the Grammy-nominated rapper, Asghedom was known not only for music but also for civic engagement— renovating a school playground, creating an incubator for young entrepreneurs. During a public memorial service at the Staples Center, attended by more than ten thousand people, a testimonial from President Obama was read aloud. "While most folks look at the Crenshaw neighborhood where he grew up and see only gangs, bullets and despair, Nipsey saw potential. He saw hope." After the service, a procession from Downtown wound its way to Crenshaw. People watched from rooftops, stood on cars under a cloudless sky and waved. Many wore blue caps, blue bandannas, blue shirts, a nod to the blue of local identity, Dodgers and Crips, but also a color signifying a greater pride, I thought, about Los Angeles south of the 10, the region's endurance despite shadeless exposure to adversity and time. I watched a man pop a wheelie on a blue motorcycle. A man rode a horse that wore a blue bandanna. "Undamaged blue, plain blue, absolutely blue, blue as a piece of roof slate" (Kate Braverman, *Lithium for Medea*).

Nearly a year later, after the death of Kobe Bryant, the city-state turned purple and gold. Bryant and his thirteen-year-old daughter, Gianna, died with seven others during a helicopter crash in Calabasas, in the San Fernando Valley. The public response was instantaneous, massive. People wept openly in the street. Murals sprang up on buildings. For weeks, Bryant's jersey was worn by grocery clerks, public librarians. The outpouring of grief seemed almost spiritually binding—Southern California, united in mourning, discussing its loss on sports radio and at family dinners. During another memorial at the Staples Center, a tearful Michael Jordan said, "When Kobe Bryant died, a piece of me died. And as I look in this arena and across the globe, a piece of you died."

During the same year, after the deaths of George Floyd and Breonna Taylor, among a long list of Black Americans killed by police—Los Angeles imploded. Months of protests and marches that were deliberately choreographed by organizers to roil neighborhoods—West Hollywood, Santa Monica—that had gone untouched in 1965 and '92. National Guard soldiers patrolled Downtown with enormous guns on their chests. One march through Hollywood was estimated to include nearly a hundred thousand people. Half a dozen helicopters swirled overhead. The protesters were from across the county, angry and frightened behind their masks—masks, worn to protect against virus spread, that on some occasions were reported to be ripped off by the police (who often were seen maskless) before people were thrown into "COVID wagons," as they became known. But the marchers were undeterred. Patrisse Cullors, an African American artist who grew up in Van Nuys, best known as one of the cofounders of Black Lives Matter, was quoted in a newspaper interview saying, "It's unheard of in L.A. to bring out 100,000 people to protest."

Cullors debuted a piece of performance art around that time called A Prayer for the Runner, saying, "There's a collective prayer. And that prayer is grounded in the idea and the belief that one day we will be free."

7.12 The murder of Victor McElhaney, I associate with the color green. Above all else, McElhaney was a musician. "He was drumming from the moment he could sit up," his mother, a city council member in Oakland, said. McElhaney studied at the Oakland Public Conservatory of Music and California State University, East Bay, before transferring to USC. In the early hours of March 10, 2019, he and a group of friends were robbed in a parking lot about a mile and a half from the university. McElhaney, a month shy of his twenty-second birthday, was shot "likely after objecting to the robbery," an LAPD captain said in a newspaper interview. Two days later, McElhaney's parents stood by a lectern at a news conference, surrounded by almost a dozen people. The curtains were beige, the flag was limp. His mother wore a flowered dress and a strand of pearls. His father wore a striped button-down shirt. University officials and employees, one after another, paid tribute to McElhaney's character, his artistry. Looking at his parents, one professor couldn't hold back his tears. McElhaney's mother said at one point, "Really I'm crying for all those who never got to meet him and know him and be touched by him."

Watching the press conference, I gasped when I recognized a young person slip behind McElhaney's mom, with their hair now dyed brightly green. "His eyes were deep," McElhaney's mother was saying about her son. "I'd always say he had something going on behind those eyes." While she said this, Bay Davis looked up and stared at the ceiling, their eyes rolling back, as if they were on the verge of passing out.

A few days later, they posted pictures online of themself and McElhaney embracing. It would appear they'd been a couple for a while, deeply in love. The caption to the photos, broken poetically with line breaks, started, "Victor McElhaney / was my partner / my love / and my friend above all else." It ended, "Victor's murder is still / under investigation / If anyone knows anything please find / the strength to come forward."

The Los Angeles City Council offered a $50,000 reward for information about the killing. The Los Angeles Board of Supervisors put up an additional $25,000. Weeks later, months later, Davis posted another picture with McElhaney, of McElhaney kissing them, cradling their head, with another poem: "I kept saying I carry / but I walk with you / I learn from you." The location stamp on the photographs put them in Oakland. I reached out, but didn't hear back, the same for later inquiries. A few months after that, a twenty-three-year-old man was charged with Victor McElhaney's murder. Two months later, I saw a photo online that showed Davis's green hair gone: they'd shaved their head and gotten the word *Victorious* tattooed on the side in large cursive lettering, looking like both a memorial and a statement, I thought, and also as if a dark feather had been tucked behind their ear.

7.13   One winter night, a London actress threw a party in a cliffside house in the Hollywood Hills. Guests sat on a white rug next to a wood-burning stove. The doorbell rang, and the actress squealed with delight when a deliveryman arrived with a large bag stained by oil, full of McDonald's fries. The actress, a short woman, recognizable from television, thrust her arm into the bag nearly all the way to the shoulder. "Oh, they're the best, you must try," she murmured. Afterward, she smoked a cigarette on the terrace. The view was grandiose and glittering. Vermont Avenue, crammed with cars all the way to Long Beach, was two long ropes of lights. "You know, L.A. isn't really a city, it's too spread out," the actress said. She shrugged and frowned. "Honestly, it's terrible. Do you know? Los Angeles magnifies everything, it really does. It completely magnifies the worst in yourself. I mean, I do love it, I love it, but I hate it." Recently, the actress had been out of work, I learned. The house atop the canyon had been borrowed from a friend. "Monday, the Emmy's, can I tell you? I was completely suicidal. All these people more successful than you, younger than you. Mental. And everyone so facetious. You want to know the city? It's addicts and storytellers, that's all." A dog trotted outside. The actress picked it up in her arms. Half Chihuahua, half pug, her "companion chug," she called it. She said in a soft voice, "I'll tell you what Los Angeles is: it's nothing. It doesn't exist."

Sometimes, when I really hated Los Angeles, I thought the actress was right. All the suffering and concrete added up to zero or less, as Bret Easton Ellis would have it—a sun-blasted nothing, a brainless amoeba with vital forces seeping in and out of the body public in some dysfunctional communion. "A place has to become an inner landscape for the imagination to start to inhabit that place, to turn it into its theatre," the Italian novelist Italo Calvino wrote when he lived in Paris. But what happened when the play was a dud? What if it was a flop?

One Sunday I attended a Gnostic rite in the dark basement rooms of a strip mall near Verdugo City. During the ceremony, each member of the congregation approached the altar to accept the Eucharist while submitting to a naked woman sitting on an altar. It was strange, though more humdrum than anything, to stand at eye level with a woman's vagina, surrounded by burning candles, and accept the blood of Jesus Christ (a shot glass of wine) and the body of Jesus Christ (a snickerdoodle, I think) and salute her womanhood. (Afterward, the clergy served a champagne brunch.) On another morning I listened to messages from outer space with the Aetherius Society, a group that believed in UFOs, and afterward they served a champagne brunch, too, but only because it was someone's birthday. And one evening, after some difficulty wrangling an invitation, I was scheduled to meet a sect of Real Vampires, or vamps—people who enjoy drinking the blood of others, or having their blood consumed—at a pizza restaurant in the Valley for happy hour, but I couldn't find them. (They look just like everybody else.) Thankfully they offered to reschedule, and we met at a bar in Hollywood, enjoyed beer and chicken wings, and I learned many things, like, "You can have a platonic donor-vamp relationship, but once you've fed two to three times, you form an intimate connection." The woman who told me this was, by day, a nurse practitioner. Her donor, sitting next to her, added, laughing, "It's because they want to play with their food."

I bring all of this up because sometimes the city-state was interminably dull but also endlessly interesting. It could feel like a hotel sometimes, like Mars sometimes, and sometimes like a hotel on Mars where Marleen Sundgaard's grandchildren lived in a furnished suite next to Elon Musk's cyborg offspring.

Los Angeles: was an exercise in horror vacui.

Los Angeles: was algae from the future.

Los Angeles: ate at the dream side of my mind.

7.14 As I looked over these propositions in aggregate, adding up the hours spent transcribing and thinking about people's feelings and thoughts, some facts became apparent, if the city-state didn't want to collapse. It needed to educate its children much better. It should become a more desirable place to do business while investing more heavily in public health and transit—affordable housing, methods of mobility, ways of sharing our richest amenities with more citizens.

Most of all, Los Angeles rapidly needed to address the breach between the wealthy and everyone else. The so-called middle class had disappeared, and a new type of feudalism seemed to be hardening into place. In the summer of 2020 the novelist Héctor Tobar wrote in an opinion piece, "I missed the earnestness and naiveté of the happy, sunburnt, flabby, and unpretentious Angeleno middle class. I missed the feeling that we were all equal, somehow: not just in the Constitutional, Enlightenment sense of that word, but also in the backyard California party sense of being comrades in relaxation gathered around barbecues and inflatable kiddie pools."

And no matter what anyone did, the basin would continue to burn, crack, and roil, and the streets again would be covered in ash. The climate crisis had us and would have us worse. Those who lived here would be weird *and* homogenized, they'd find their surroundings inspiring *and* despairing. And for at least a little while longer, to its credit, Los Angeles would remain North America's eclectic doom-brain plasticity test, where so much was still up for grabs: a reverie on demographics and cultural trends; the final acts of a play about the villainies of property-based politics; a road crew working on the future where almost anybody could grab a shovel. "This is where you come if you want to have one foot on solid ground and one foot on ground that shakes a lot," the cultural historian and USC professor Josh Kun told me. "There's an edginess here that's geological, psychological, and creative. You can have a freedom here that you might not be able to have in other places in the U.S. If that means you're living in your own country, I think there's something to that."

This book never intended to wear a Dodger cap. The history of Los Angeles doesn't lack for boosters, and depictions continue to be overly optimistic or pessimistic. Disasters—pandemics, earthquakes—pause human time, and the lucky survive. Our health was improving; our health was critical. The smog had improved and then begun to slip drastically, especially in neighborhoods that weren't wealthy. Meanwhile, housing costs had gotten so high, residents were among the United States' most cost burdened. "We've been a city of houses, and we've abandoned the majority of our population to being housing precarious, housing-burdened, or homeless," Dana Cuff, the architecture theorist at UCLA, told me. "Our schoolteachers can't afford to be here—there's something fundamentally wrong about that."

A place of layers. A place of palimpsest. A place of loss.

To paraphrase the Swedish statistician Hans Rosling, the existence of the city-state often seemed to be "better and bad" at the same time, was how I'd come to think of it. Or, as the *Los Angeles Times* columnist Steve Lopez put it in the paper one morning, "Los Angeles is a singular, inspired mess, paradise lost and found, prone to natural catastrophe and too chaotic and leaderless to be neatly assessed as getting better or worse. It's always doing some of both, and like any work in progress, it's in greater need of critics than defenders."

7.15 Sometimes "better and bad" was most evident when a long effort at justice was accomplished. On an autumn morning, one of the city-state's most notorious criminals sat through his sentencing trial. Downtown, on the stuffy ninth floor of the Clara Shortridge Foltz Criminal Justice Center, maybe half a dozen reporters were in the first row of a wood-paneled courtroom while the next row overflowed with family members of the victim, Terry Carter, known as "Pops," killed in 2015 at the age of fifty-five. And in the final two rows were what seemed to be friends and relatives of the defendant, fewer in number despite his fame. The defendant's father appeared to sit in front of me, the defendant's sister next to me—both identifications based on photos I quickly found with my phone. Nearby sat a young man with a cursive tattoo on his neck: KNIGHTLIFE.

"We've been here ninety-three days, make this ninety-four days," one of Carter's daughters said. That morning was the trial's final get-together, and the victim's family had been invited to offer impact statements. Members were told to direct their comments to the judge, not the accused, who sat nearby in an orange jumpsuit, though most of their comments sounded meant for the accused, and some were addressed that way. "You don't run over somebody and run back over them and not know what you're doing," Carter's brother-in-law said at one point. One relative read aloud from a letter written by Carter's wife. "'When my husband's name is Googled, you don't see videos of our wedding,'" he read. "'What you do see is the defendant kill my husband.'"

Carter was described in the newspaper as a paternal figure, helping young men avoid gang life. The defendant, Marion Hugh "Suge" Knight Jr., represented a glorification of gang culture, in a way that had enriched him while being marketed to millions. One relative talked about the violence the defendant had done conceptually to Los Angeles, specifically to Compton, the Carters' city within the city, which the accused had helped make famous in his image. Family members said the defendant hadn't even apologized to them, hadn't shown remorse. "I hope and I pray that we can find forgiveness," one of Carter's cousins said, "but it won't be today."

Carter's death took place at a branch of Tam's Burgers, a local fast-food chain, on Rosecrans Avenue. Knight had been in a fight with another man, allegedly tried to drive him over with his truck, and struck Carter instead. In the courthouse, the judge assigned Knight twenty-eight years. The woman near me, whom I took to be his sister, said quietly, "Oh no . . ." An hour later, the atmosphere at Tam's was quiet. A man in a business suit ate a burrito. A work crew in reflective vests ate burgers and fries. Compton lay low under bright sunlight. Businesses were busy, lawns were kept. A young man with a towel over his shoulder pushed a baby carriage and nodded when I passed. The Pacific Ocean lapped endlessly some twelve miles west.

"You know, the biggest misconception is when America looks at these people, they think it's all just one personality," Kendrick Lamar, the Compton local and Pulitzer Prize–winning rapper, said in a 2016 documentary. "It is a sense of optimism. It's moving forward in certain directions. I think a lot of kids out here, they recognize the talent and the potential that we all have."

7.16   What can be said of the United States often can be said most clearly about Los Angeles. Historically, the city-state had often suggested where not only the American city was headed but also the American people, with all their Americanness. All gig workers now, all climate refugees now. All of us trapped, consciously or not, by our racist past and policies. It is probably too soon to know, but perhaps the coronavirus outbreak of 2020 will be a catalyst for other cities to grow more nationlike and challenge the primacy of the state as the era of globalism disintegrates and power devolves to local levels.

"I absolutely think of Los Angeles as a city-state," Mayor Eric Garcetti told me. "The root of *politics* is the same as the root word in Greek for *city, polis*. People engage in politics because they came to a city and vice versa. There's no question that we are a city state, even though we chop ourselves up in a confusing way."

At the same time, Los Angeles was not the United States in miniature, like Houston, Chicago, or New York. Always an invented city, L.A. was creating a new type of city-state as we watched, internet version or otherwise, one that would yield to time and manipulation and social clash, of course, but also would offer a study on what tomorrow's communal urban living might look like. If anything, as the century approached its quarter mark, Los Angeles felt to my mind like the rawest, large-scale example still running of the American experiment—a self-made place attracting self-made people, though one where diversity and dispersion were significant assets, not figments of a dream. "It's really more unusual than common that people from radically different backgrounds share a society together peacefully," Kit Rachlis, the magazine editor, told me. "Other cities have their many layers of immigrants, too. But in L.A., not only are we all connected; we are also part of this large experiment. New York, Paris, Chicago, those places are still changing, but the pace is slow and the people who change them are encrusted. Here, there's a sense that any of us could change it. That's pretty wonderful."

Under the soft SoCal light, small differences dissolved, car stereos throbbed, a sense of tension persisted from monotony and difference sitting side by side.

Rachlis's comment echoed something that Jade Chang, the novelist from Northridge, once told me: Los Angeles is a place where people get to choose their own experience. If you're in the middle of Manhattan, you walk out the door "and the city is right in front of you, take it or leave it." But in the city-state, she felt, you could make a life where you lived in a canyon, and that was it, or on a block in East L.A. that you never left—wherever you were, there was your piece of the polycentrism, enclaved.

7.17 If there is a predominant feeling in the city-state, it is not loneliness or daze, but an uneasy temporariness, a sense of life's impermanence: the tension of anticipation while so much quivers on the line. Ethnic division, ethnic celebration. Haves, have-nots. Industrial decline, industrial revival. Terror of plague and fear of earthquake, but also the comfort of seeing neighbors help neighbors in Skid Row. For all of L.A.'s apparent selfishness, benevolence seemed to be a local trait. At rush hour one afternoon, on a 780 bus from Olympic to Pasadena, 75 percent of passengers thanked the driver before they disembarked. The next day, on the 110, one driver let another pass, and both waved. At Dodger Stadium, during the coronavirus pandemic, while one of its massive parking lots was converted into what was possibly the world's largest free testing and vaccination center for

COVID-19—staffed largely by volunteers from a nonprofit agency co-founded, in a particularly Hollywood-ish twist, by the actor Sean Penn—person after person thanked the volunteers for playing their part.

Nothing is fixed. Each evening unveils yet one more hypnotic sunset, and still L.A. remains a "provisional city," in the words of Dana Cuff, so old but young, same-seeming but miscellaneous, planned but given to chance, with more to come.

Nearly a decade before moving to California, Rachel and I lived in France, where I listened to episodes of *Good Food*, a radio show produced by KCRW in Santa Monica. At the time, I had few connections with Los Angeles, but I loved the conversations between the host, chef Evan Kleiman, and a local food writer, Jonathan Gold. Gold wasn't yet the first food critic to win a Pulitzer Prize, but a writer known for crisscrossing L.A. County in search of great meals. And it was the way that he talked about the region, rather than its restaurants, that made me want to visit—the idea that Los Angeles was a vast kingdom of vast interest. Kleiman once said in an interview in the newspaper, "Do you know how many people have told me that when they moved here, they had no idea how to deal with Los Angeles? And they used [Gold] as a template to learn the city. It made them flip from being afraid and kind of not happy to be here to embracing it."

Gold died from pancreatic cancer in 2018 at the age of fifty-seven. The day after, I drove around Los Angeles to eat three of his favorite Mexican dishes: smoked marlin tacos in Inglewood, a shrimp taco in Boyle Heights, the clayuda at an Oaxacan restaurant in Koreatown. At the last stop, a family of tourists speaking French waited by the valet stand. It was their first time visiting, the father said. They loved the beaches, the different neighborhoods, the variety of people. "It's, how do you say, just so American." I was reminded of how even France had felt the same that year, when Le Bon Marché, the grand Parisian department store, had designed its annual Christmas theme around a Southern California aesthetic, complete with vintage motorcycles and a skateboard ramp. "We used to hear a lot about New York in the past," Jennifer Cuvillier, the store's fashion director, said. "Now it's more and more about Los Angeles."

7.18   One final story, because no one remembers Nathan K. Mendelsohn. Mendelsohn, called Nat, who wore white gloves and a homburg hat, was one of America's biggest dreamers, yet his legacy today is apparition-like: no park so christened, no biography written, just California City, a desert community about a hundred miles north of Dodger Stadium that is surrounded by a matrix of empty streets, grids upon grids that look from a plane as if they were tattooed on the land by a civilization that once loomed colossal, then ghosted us without a trace, as if a family of tornadoes had swept across a sand empire of several million people and ripped up King Mendelsohn and his court, along with every building, bulldozer, and shrieking child, and violently funneled them away, leaving behind only the crop circles of vanished suburbia.

No one today knew Mendelsohn's name, not because he failed to achieve his dream, but because so few people had chosen to share it.

"An expert in population trends, Professor Nathan Mendelsohn of Columbia University predicted that the

Los Angeles basin could not contain the increased population and laid out his model community, California City, to catch the overflow," *Life* magazine reported in 1962. That was roughly four years after Mendelsohn had started cutting roads in the Mojave Desert to build the next great American metropolis. One new resident remarked to the *Life* reporter, "I can't say exactly why, but once it takes a hold, a man has a tough time being happy anywhere else."

About sixty years later, California City was the third-largest city in California, going by area, but the town was a mere outpost: about fourteen thousand residents, not including the desert tortoises or a few thousand prison inmates. And then, sprawling out into the wilderness, a massive ghost network of roads and sand dunes, with at least one dune that was much steeper than it originally appeared over the hood of a Honda Accord.

Mendelsohn was born in 1915. According to his obituary, he was prototypical of the kind of people who wound up in Southern California—an immigrant, a former East Coaster, a visionary determined to see his fantasy realized. And his particular fantasy was that the desert could become home to the never-ending development the city-state seemed to incubate. "When Mendelsohn first pitched California City, he saw it as a rival to L.A., even bigger than L.A.," Geoff Manaugh, the architectural writer, told me. "It was inspired by the greater sprawl of L.A., to make something even bigger."

Bank loans allowed Mendelsohn to construct cul de sacs and name streets for Stanford and Yale. He imagined a grand "Central Park," inspired by Manhattan's Central Park, with a lake rippled by desert winds; for the opening ceremony, water reportedly was flown all the way from New

York. An advertising jingle at the time said it all: "Buy a piece of the Golden State. You'll be sitting pretty when you come to California City." Lots hit the market in 1958. Buses rolled in with customers, and loudspeakers proclaimed each sale, with a new three-bedroom house starting at $8,700. Still, around the time of the *Life* article, few homes had been constructed. Most lots were sold for speculation. Seven years after opening, the population of California City would number less than two thousand—sprawl actually *had* hit a wall, and soon Mendelsohn himself would sell his stake, tip his hat, and depart for other projects. He died in 1984 in Texas, where he'd worked on developing another community.

It was two, three o'clock on a weekday when I stuck my car into the sand dune. The sun was a shimmering white. The temperature was supposed to hit 100 degrees. I checked my phone: no service. For at least an hour, I hadn't seen a single other car on the grid, no humans except an outlying dirt-bike rider *braap-braaping*. Surrounded by mountains and a sustained chord of sand, so much sand, with the nearest paved road about a mile away, it was around then I realized I hadn't packed any extra water in the car.

This is how people in the desert sometimes die, I thought.

If Greater L.A. were a city-state, then California City was its acid jam—Los Angeles exaggerated, Los Angeles stripped naked, Los Angeles the IMAX movie flattened to AM radio. "It's like the painting in *The Picture of Dorian Gray*," Manaugh told me. "You've got this place that tried to be like Los Angeles, totally failed, and became the voodoo version." The desert that made up L.A.'s hinterlands was where Elon Musk and others were working on ways to send humans into outer space. Friends who lived in the town of Desert Hot Springs told me about the night the gasoline was stolen out of their truck—not siphoned off, but someone crawled under their pickup and detached the gas tank and ran away. And the desert was where, higher and drier, asylum seekers had been known to wait miserably in Adelanto's U.S. Immigration and Customs Enforcement (ICE) Processing Center, a privately run detention facility that resembled from the road a big-box store painted beige, as if to match the sand and operate in camouflage—a place where Osmar Epifanio Gonzalez-Gadba, a thirty-two-year-old Nicaraguan man, died in 2017, found hanging from his bedsheets. During an inspection a year later, officials discovered nooses hanging from vents in fifteen of twenty cells.

In California City, the failed metropolis, for several hours before my Honda Accord got stuck in the sand, a handful of local citizens complained to me about a lack of jobs. They worked in a dusty village adjacent to a geoglyph. Their neighbors commuted to solar fields, a borax mine, an air force base, then returned home to mute streets. A young waitress at the Coyote Café murmured, "We don't even have a bowling alley." None of them had heard of Nat Mendelsohn, but they knew his roads, and also about the roads' repurposing, telling me that for decades and to this day, tens of thousands of people would arrive in town around Thanksgiving weekend, towing motorbikes and other desert toys to party on the giant earthwork. A California City police officer said that the crowds got so big, they sometimes employed a helicopter to run patrols. Also, there was the cannabis industry: in 2017, the former boxer Mike Tyson broke ground on "Tyson Ranch," dedicated to growing, selling, and promoting weed. At the time, the mayor of California City called the Tyson development "a rebirth for the entire city." Also, there was Wasteland Weekend: thousands of postapocalyptic types arriving dressed up like they were auditioning for *Mad Max*, to enjoy a Burning Man–style circus of gladiator fights.

"It's a weird place," Manaugh told me. He had also driven up before to roam the sand. "There's nothing to see, but that's the point. What's interesting is that what's there is what you bring with you. California City rewards people who approach it with an imaginative sense of what it can be."

"It sounds like you're describing Los Angeles," I said.

"Absolutely I am," he said.

The city-state wasn't a jumble of people any more than a song was a string of notes. Los Angeles spoke. Los Angeles wept. Los Angeles *exuded*. I went to the desert to understand the city-state better and slammed my car into a wall of sand—how's that for a metaphor. But after a lot of rocking and sweating, finally able to drive home, I couldn't shake the feeling that California City, through allegory, through necromancy, suggested its own metaphor of what Los Angeles might become if it failed: not the ceaseless night of *Blade Runner*, but the brown noise of the desert, an echo of an interval briefly realized before cleansings by drought and time.

Where there was nothing to see and everything to do.

Where only some people were unrestricted, fewer were deeply rooted, and many felt emptiness in their lives, broken apart from one another.

Where history repeated itself daily, no matter that what happened a few blocks away might as well have taken place in Madagascar.

Where the risks were enormous and the rewards reached only a few.

Frequently, cities bypass their nations on critical issues. All around the world, there was a sense early in the century that we lived in the prehistory of a new age, and here came Los Angeles: a shifting mosaic of human potential. An all-hours diner, real, surreal, so real. "Let Pauline be Irene. Let you be Beeton. And let me be Los Angeles" (James Joyce, *Finnegans Wake*). Gone was the suburban era, expansion was limited while blocks stratified, and yes, the city-state continued to offer, for those who might cast it as a microcosm of the United States, probably the best place to watch America unfold before we all permanently moved onto the internet. But it was so much more than that—no other place quite so thrillingly itself, with so many stories lying around untouched. "There are a lot of things that are true of Los Angeles that are also true of other American cities," Héctor Tobar told me. "But in no other American cities are those truths as evident as they are in Los Angeles."

"The thing that people find hard to understand, I think, is sort of the magnitude of what's here," Jonathan Gold says at one point in *City of Gold*, a documentary about his life. "The huge number of multiple cultures that live in the city who come together in this beautiful and haphazard fashion. And the fault lines between them are sometimes where you find the most beautiful things."

7.19 Sometimes, in Los Angeles, it felt like time had stopped but life kept going. Sometimes it felt like time was rushing by and the end was near. Sometimes it felt like both things simultaneously—life pulsing, time rushing—with everything under the sun here all at once, and still low-key.

"There comes a time when the sun is defiant," the East

L.A. writer Helena María Viramontes wrote in her story "The Moths." "Just about the time when moods change, inevitable seasons of a day, transitions from one color to another, that hour or minute or second when the sun is finally defeated, finally sinks into the realization that it cannot with all its power to heal or burn, exist forever . ..."

Los Angeles is Los Angeles. Temporary, total, incomplete. Another morning dawns. The air is soft while the fog burns off. Somewhere, a bougainvillea flowers.

So be it! See to it!

The city-state wakes.

ACKNOWLEDGMENTS

My gratitude goes out: to my editor and publisher, Sean McDonald. His vision and sustained encouragement, also his passion for Southern California, are a major part of why this book exists.

To my literary agent, PJ Mark, for many things, but a long friendship most of all.

To all the unmentioned conversation partners, early readers, door openers, moral supporters, cottage loaners: Tim Adams, Matthew Aselton, Graham Beck, Blake Berris, J.B., Steph Cha, Nalleli Cobo, Alex Creasia, William Deverell, Fred and Sarah Doering, Jack Dolman, Amina Fields, Amelia Gray, Daniel Hernandez, Woodwyn Koons, Sara Lamm, Juliet Lapidos, G.L., Mirra Levitt, R.M., Kelly McEvers, Alexandra McGuinness, Julia Meltzer, Victor Quinaz, Tejal Rao, Davy Rothbart, Sam Sanders, Stephanie Schwam, Lee Shipman, Dmitri Siegel, Lydia Turner, Monic Uriarte, Brendan Vaughan, Mark Wheeler, Lopez Williams, Charles Yu.

To the many great editors, art directors, and fact-checkers at GQ who permitted me to turn wanderings for this book into features along the way, most of all Geoff Gagnon and Daniel Riley, legends.

To the librarians at the Los Angeles Public Library, especially the dedicated staff of the Los Feliz branch, and also Glen Creason, Ann Burroughs at the Japanese American National Museum, Adam Murray at the Inner City Law Center, Natalie Russell at the Huntington Library, and Kate Hutton at the Emergency Management Department. Also, to Ryan Cowen at the U.S. Department of Agriculture, who knows cattle.

To the Los Angeles publications and people who do the hard work, from indies to bigs, and offer so much inspiration: *All Night Menu, Desert Oracle,* KCRW, KPCC, *LAist, L.A. Taco, L.A. Weekly* (RIP), *The LAnd Magazine, Los Angeles Magazine,* the *Los Angeles Sentinel,* the *Los Angeles Times, Rafu Shimpo.* To the countless local writers and artists. To everyone who fed me tacos. To the agitators, social workers, firefighters, bus drivers, nonprofit employees, arts organizations—anybody working day in, day out to improve the lives of Angelenos. John and LaRee Caughey write at the end of *Los Angeles: Biography of a City* (1977), "Pessimists and optimists agree that if life in Los Angeles is not made better, it will become worse." Yup.

Finally, to those appearing in this book who shared their ideas and stories with me and endured my visits, questions, and early-morning or late-night texts, you have my apologies for any errors, and most of all my immeasurable gratitude.

Most of all to Rachel Knowles, my love, for everything.